BITCOIN, ETH CRYPTOCURRE.... .... AND INVESTING FOR BEGINNERS

What To Do With Privacy Coins And Smart Contract Blockchains In 2022 And Beyond

Herman Moss

TABLE OF CONTENTS

INTRODUCTION

This book focuses on bitcoin, Ethereum, privacy coins, and smart contract blockchain investment and trading, revealing many tactics and strategies. First, you'll learn about the finest cryptocurrencies to trade with and how to trade ether futures. Following that, you will discover how to maximize your gains during the Bull Run and how to invest in cryptocurrency responsibly. You'll also learn how to invest in and trade Cardano and Polkadot, as well as how to save money on ethereum gas fees. You will also discover the principles of bitcoin investment, the future of bitcoin mining, and how much to invest in bitcoin versus ethereum. Following that, you will discover how to trade utilizing FTX, Huobi, and BNB tokens, as well as which privacy coins, Oracle cryptos, and smart contract blockchains to invest in and trade with. Finally, you will discover how to keep your crypto assets secure in the short and long term. If you're ready to dive in, let's start with the best 5 altcoins to invest in and trade in 2022 and beyond.

CHAPTER 1:

WHAT ARE THE BEST ALTCOINS TO TRADE WITH

Without a question, we look to be in the midst of the next crypto bull run. Bitcoin is nearing all-time highs, and the market looks to be on the verge of breaking some extremely exciting records. This is not just beneficial to Bitcoin, but it is also beneficial to the altcoin market. Those who have been following the crypto markets for a while would know that when Bitcoin has rebounded, there is always a shift to altcoins. However, considering how sophisticated the markets have gotten, this rising tide is unlikely to raise all boats. Only a few cryptocurrencies are likely to capture the benefits you want. This raises an essential question: which ones? That's exactly what I'm going to talk about in this chapter. I'll walk you through five of my top cryptocurrency predictions for 2022. Picks that are not only well-diversified in terms of technology, market cap, and use cases but also all coins that have the potential to skyrocket next year. It's worth giving you a brief rundown of how I picked these options. It's a significant insight into how I think about portfolio diversity and allocation in general. I approach coin selection in the same way as I approach my portfolio. It all comes down to diversity. Diversification in terms of underlying use cases, market capitalization, and sector. This is significant because, regardless of how fantastic a project appears on paper, the industry in which it operates may not be as hot. However, by selecting projects from various industries, you are diversifying your sector risk. Another factor that I attempt to balance is the market capitalization of the coins on the list. Some of these options, as you'll see, have a very big market cap among the top 50, but others are more of your moonshots with market values below the top 200.

This is significant since you will know that the possibilities of achieving a 50x return on a token are significantly higher on a low cap jewel than on a promising but big market cap currency. Why? Well, arithmetic, but low-cap coins are inherently riskier and more volatile. The chance of the token going through the floor is greater in smaller initiatives than in larger and more established ones. It's also worth noting that these are presented in no particular sequence below, so don't read too much into that. But, whatever you do, please try to understand why I picked each of these coins. Monero is my first choice. Aside from having the most advanced cryptographic protocols on the market, it also represents something much more basic in terms of financial independence. Satoshi's vision: truly anonymous peer-to-peer digital currency. It's very well-established crypto that's been around for approximately six years, but it's been in the headlines a lot recently due to who has it in their sights. After all, the powers that be aren't too thrilled about complete financial independence. I'm referring to prosecutors, regulators, and other significant law enforcement agencies with three letter abbreviations. As a result, it's evident that Monero has some formidable adversaries, and you may be asking how on earth I can include it on my list. One man's meat is another man's poison, as they say.

These agencies' extreme emphasis, in my opinion, demonstrates that they see Monero privacy-enhancing technology as a danger. A menace that they are unable to contain. This can only suggest that it is functioning as designed, and despite having so much thrown at it by all of these parties, they have yet to crack the encryption and de-anonymize people. Ciphertrace has a patent that aids with transaction tracking, although it is merely a probabilistic approach. It employs well-known transaction clustering techniques to zero down on plausible address flows, but it is still a long way from breaking the algorithm. Apart from that, there are a lot of additional reasons why I am so optimistic about Monero. First and foremost, as previously said, the privacy technology is unparalleled. Second, while engineers try to strengthen the protocol and ensure its anonymity, this technology is continually changing. Speaking about those developers, they are among the most fervent cypherpunks in the crypto field.

A larger group of idealistic people who are all motivated by the desire to keep their financial independence. I should also note out that all R&D financing on the Monero network comes from the community, with no outside sponsorship. Another reason I prefer

Monero over other privacy currencies is that it has the most liquidity among them. This is despite the fact that anonymity has been placed under assault on exchanges by default currencies such as Monero. The truth is that Monero is still a popular cryptocurrency. There will always be a demand for it and an exchange eager to serve it, and even if centralized exchanges make using trading XMR difficult, decentralized alternatives will soon fill the void. That's because XMR-BTC atomic swaps are one of the most exciting community-funded R&D projects being worked on right now. This will make it possible for users to effortlessly trade Monero for Bitcoin and vice versa via the blockchain.

A smooth transition from where the all-seeing eye rules to where it is blind. It's also worth noting that Monero is one of the more decentralized proof-of-work cryptocurrencies. This is due to a number of adjustments made to its mining algorithm. As you are no doubt aware, centralization is one of the most serious threats to a distributed system. There are several concerns about the concentration of Bitcoin's mining hash rate in China, for example. Finally, I believe in Monero because of the current situation of the world. If there is one recurring theme this year, it is that privacy is under attack, from anti-encryption legislation to forced exchange reporting requirements, from the abolition of cash to the introduction of central bank digital currencies. As more people understand that their liberties are being trampled on, they will gravitate toward remedies that protect those liberties. Monero was the name. Algorand is the next selection. We're all aware that there's a lot of buzz surrounding smart contract blockchains, so look no further than the excitement surrounding Ethereum 2.0. However, one size does not fit all, and it will not be a winner-take-all situation. As a result, it may be prudent to diversify your allocation to other developer-friendly blockchains.

There are several potential networks out there, but Algorand is one that has been on my radar for quite some time. Let's start with a high-level summary. Algorand is a blockchain that has set out to actively address the well-known blockchain trilemma. They aspire to create a blockchain that is scalable, safe, and decentralized. It is up to their very efficient consensus mechanism to figure out how they want to do this. It's known as pure evidence of stake. The key advantage is that Algorand's technology finalizes blocks in seconds and delivers instant transaction finality while preventing forks. Why am I so optimistic about Algorand? So, let's begin from the beginning. This project's personnel reads like a who's who of encryption. It is made up of some of the brightest minds in the area from colleges such as MIT. The originator is a professor named Silvio McCarley, who is well-known for being the first to provide zero knowledge proofs. That core technology is mentioned in so many cryptocurrency ventures. He earned a Turing Award for his work on this, but it's not only intellectual power that's supporting the initiative. It also has a lot of money. Algorand really has a distinct venture capital arm that has secured a significant amount of investment for the development and adoption of companies built on Algorand. Consider it akin to Ethereum consensus or Emurgo on Cardano. This Algorand company has already spawned a number of companies, and as we all know, adoption is critical to a blockchain's utility demand. In terms of acceptance, the USDC stablecoin has recently been merged onto the Algorand network.

This implies that USDC users will be able to transmit the stablecoin on the Algorand network for less money and faster than they would on Ethereum. It's also no secret that USDC is quickly becoming the world's de facto stablecoin. For example, you may have heard the recent historic announcement that Visa will be giving USDC settlement to all of its 60 million merchants. All of this transaction demand will necessitate the use of a very fast and efficient blockchain. All of this transaction demand on Algorand will inevitably result in a demand to pay for the transactions that are paid in Algo. While we're on the issue of blockchain utility demand, I should also mention that Algorand is actively courting the DeFi sector with their unique smart contract language called Teal. It's a non-turing complete language that, although limiting capabilities, is typically seen to be safer to create and run. Perhaps it might be an appealing option for corporate developers concerned about the stability of smart contracts, for example. Algorand is excellent, but why is the pricing so low? Well, I believe that is primarily due to an initial excess from the IPO last year. They appeared to have sold quite a deal in the early auctions, and when they were released to the market, the price plummeted. They have, however, conducted a number of buybacks and revamped its tokenomics. I should also mention that it is a staking blockchain, which implies that the more staked, the less circulating supply there is, all of which is price accretive. As a result, Algorand might be an appealing smart contract play in 2022. Theta, the next token, is a project that aims to totally alter how we think about streaming and online video distribution. They particularly aim to decentralize and democratize it, and the Theta blockchain is the market's only end-to-end infrastructure for decentralized video streaming and distribution.

This kind of scale is made possible by some really amazing streaming and blockchain technologies. I'd want to focus on why I believe theta might be such a popular selection for 2022. To begin, streaming is extremely popular, as seen by the billions of users on YouTube and Twitch. Because these are all on centralized platforms and employ centralized content delivery networks, it's easy to understand why Theta is intriguing in this context. Theta, on the other hand, is genuinely streaming material. They began with E-sports but have now expanded to Poker, Cryptocurrency events, and have teamed with MGM to momentarily stream Hollywood classics. You can also add the SpaceX launch and K-pop events to that list. I'd also want to point out that Theta has an excellent staff and even better advisers. Among them are Stephen Chen, the founder of YouTube, and Justin Kan, the founder of Twitch. Theta has also attracted funding from companies such as Samsung. I should also mention that Theta Labs received a US patent in September 2020 for its decentralized blockchain streaming technology, which is technically titled "Methods and systems for a decentralized data streaming and delivery network." Patents aid in the security of business models. When it comes to Theta tokenomics, there are two tokens to consider: Theta and Theta fuel. Theta has a limited quantity, and all tokens are currently in circulation. This implies you won't face any dumping from investors or team members.

Also, 55 percent of all theta tokens are staked, implying that there is less token supply on the market. Staking these Theta coins will yield you Theta fuel or Tfuel. T-fuel is used as smart contract gas and will be permanently destroyed once used, so you will not only be able to own and stake rare and limited Theta tokens, but you will also earn T-fuel tokens, which should become more valuable over time as they are burned, assuming protocol inflation does not outweigh it. Another thing to keep in mind from the standpoint of utility demand is that Theta smart contracts will be interoperable with Ethereum. This means that Theta might bring in some of the hot DeFi taste that Ethereum has received in 2020. This utility demand might increase pricing, and there's another factor in the works that could push up the Theta price. That might be a Coinbase listing. Theta was added to the exchange's list of tokens that they are contemplating listing in July 2020, and we all know the impact of the historic Coinbase pump. As a result, I believe Theta might be an appealing and varied investment for your 2022 portfolio. Let's go on to my next recommendation, which is a medium-cap coin called Injective protocol. The Injective protocol is a Cosmos-based decentralized derivatives exchange. It was one of the most anticipated Dex debuts this year, and it has already gained a lot of traction.

They are attempting to bring about a paradigm shift in the deck space. Simply said, it will let users to trade spot, swaps, and futures without requiring any permissions. They will also be able to structure and advertise their own derivatives on the site. Users may someday be able to create their own decentralized derivative contracts for anything that has a price. Technically, it is constructed with Ethermint and implemented as a Cosmos SDK module. This essentially implies that it has one significant edge over the majority of Ethereum-based Dexes on the market: throughput. This is due to the fact that it is a tier 2 Cosmos zone and hence does not have to deal with the congestion that other Ethereum-based Dexes have. Furthermore, because it is based on Cosmos, it allows you to swap more than simply ERC20 assets. This is due to the nature of how Cosmos stones function. Instead of a single blockchain, there are a number of interconnected and autonomous blockchains. Clearly, I am optimistic about the technology underlying the Injective protocol, but there are a number of additional reasons why it is one to keep an eye on in 2022. To begin, Injective Labs is supported by some well-known venture capitalists in the field. Pantera Capital and Binance are two examples. Second, the crew is highly accomplished, and they've been working on the protocol for quite some time, dating back to 2018. They recently launched their solstice test net, and it's looking well. This testnet launch sparked a lot of excitement in the community. It also received some media attention, with reports appearing on sites such as Techcrunch and Cointelegraph.

However, this was only the opening volley, as the injective team recently published version two of their test net only eight days after version one. If all goes as planned on the test net, we should expect a much-anticipated mainnet debut in 2022. In terms of the INJ token itself. It really contains some very good tokenomics. There was only a little fraction; approximately 9% of the overall supply. It was in such strong demand in the IEO that the price instantly surged once trading began. I also don't think any of those private sale or founder tokens will flood the market anytime soon. This is due to the fact that the token unlock timetable looks to be pretty acceptable. Once the main net is operational, these tokens will be used to pay transaction fees. These fees are subsequently burnt, resulting in a decrease in circulating supply. At that point, tokens are removed from the market and staked on the network, and you have two variables that are long-term price positive. That doesn't even take into account the possible demand for holding the token in order to participate in decentralized governance. As we've seen in the DeFi space, the ability to participate in the protocol's decentralized governance is a significant valuation indicator in the token. Aside from that, INJ has a lot more upside potential than the previous three options due to its market cap. Smaller cap coins are likely to have higher return multiples, and speaking of market cap, it's time to disclose my 2022 micro cap moonshot choice. Barnbridge is a DeFi project with an incredible protocol. Essentially, it is a project that seeks to tokenize risk. What exactly do I mean? In the DeFi space, they're attempting to isolate and tokenize various yield risks. It operates essentially by collecting cash on the network and then assigning these amounts to various DeFi protocols. These include Arve, Compound DyDx, Synthetics, and others. After the funds have been withdrawn, the yield will be tranched so that it may be tokenized separately. As a result, DeFi clients can participate in different risk tranches based on their yield and risk tolerance.

This is known as their smart yield product, and it was the first one they released. They are, however, working on a comparable device called Smart Alpha. This will be more complicated and will be focused on splitting token returns into distinct risk tranches rather than just tranching DeFi yield or interest. Essentially, risk exposure will be derived from pricing rather than yield. All you need to know is that it's a one-of-a-kind endeavor in the DeFi space. It will not only match users to their desired risk tranches, but it will also allow users to invest in fixed interest rate DeFi instruments with certainty around that yield. So, why am I so optimistic about Barnbridge? For starters, it's perfectly positioned to capitalize on the enormous developments in DeFi that we're witnessing. In 2020, the entire value locked within DeFi technologies went parabolic, and I don't expect it to slow down in 2022. Given the unique nature of Barnbridge's protocol, it is expected to be far more appealing than any other loan platform and Dex protocols. Second, the project has received backing from the founders of both Arve and

Synthetics, who no doubt know a thing or two about developing a DeFi protocol. They only received a little amount of initial seed money and had a really successful protocol launch. There will be no ICO, and the community will get 68 percent of the bond token through a variety of yield farming and liquidity incentives. These governance tokens will subsequently be utilized on the platform to vote on critical governance issues. There are plans in the works to ultimately issue smart contracts regulated by the DAO in which users may decide what the core contracts should perform. This means that Barnbridge residents may have a vote in how risk is tranched and which processes are invested in. In the same way that Wi-Fi token holders make economic decisions that advance the entire yearn finance platform forward, bond token holders will be able to do the same, adding fundamental value to the token. Aside from that, we can simply examine the broader tokenomics. There will never be more than 10 million bond tokens released. You won't be able to mine any more of it after they've been entirely dispersed, which will take roughly two to three years. As a result, you have an asset that has a naturally restricted supply. Consider Yearn Finance; after that 30,000 Wi-Fi tokens were released, they were rather valuable. Furthermore, the Barnbridge community appears to be quite invested in the project, with 200 million USD already locked into the protocol two days after it went online. The developers are also hard at work on such financing products, which are expected to be live in the coming months. If these items live up to expectations, I have a hunch Barnbridge will be a DeFi favorite in 2022.

When it comes to bond tokens, they are presently exclusively accessible for trade on Uniswap. However, if you have some free stablecoin capital, you could join their liquidity pools and farm some bonds. Given the bond's present low market capitalization, the upside potential from here is pretty significant. Of course, I'll qualify everything by saying that this is still a novel process, and as such, there are dangers. That concludes my top five selections for 2022. As I indicated at the outset, they were carefully picked to provide a well-diversified cryptocurrency play for 2022, therefore I would advise against investing all in one of these specific projects. You expose yourself to idiosyncratic risks that cannot be simply hedged away. I'll also add that this isn't the only coin or token I'm interested in for 2022. There are several other intriguing ideas in which I am confident, and you should be as well!

CHAPTER 2:

HOW TO TRADE ETHER FUTURES

A long-term outlook on Ethereum's potential Of course, as soon as the market began to flip in late January, these ICO teams began dumping their tokens. Add to that the fact that retail investors were not as keen to enter the ICO markets as they had been in the past. There is a flood of supply with a considerably lower demand. As a result, the price of Eth plummeted all the way to zero. At the end of the year, it had dropped to around 91 dollars. Not ideal if you were one of the handful who purchased near the top. With Eth now approaching 1.8K, a crucial concern arises: may something similar occur? For a variety of reasons, this is quite improbable. Let us begin with the most fundamental of all: who is buying? While the 2017 surge was mostly fueled by retail buyers, it appears that this time around the buyers are deep-pocketed institutions and whales. These traditional financiers are hoping to profit from other digital assets. They've gone down the rabbit hole of Ethereum now that they fully grasp the value proposition of Bitcoin, and they're embracing what they're finding. I can provide a lot of data points, but let's start with one of the most well-known. Greyscale's holdings of Ether. Greyscale is a global asset management trust firm that provides institutional investors with crypto-backed shares. They have noticed an increase in the quantity of Eth required by their investors over the last year. This has, of course, meant that they have had to acquire more Eth from the market in order to retain it in their coffers. In May of 2020, for example, there were around 210 million dollars in Eth in the Greyscale funds.

They had issued somewhat more than 13.5 million Greyscale shares. How do those figures look now? Each has over 3 billion dollars and over 295 million shares. Those Greyscale investors had clearly been chowing down. According to Grayscale Investments' managing director in a Bloomberg interview, "there's a growing conviction around Ethereum as an asset class." Even more intriguing is the fact that he sees these as a new type of investor that is "Ethereum first." Not only are these investors enamored with Ethereum, but they are primarily interested in Ether. Grayscale is the only company that sells shares in its fund. What about those who purchase on the open market and stack? Well, we can look at some onchain data to get an idea of it. Sentiment's chart essentially examines the wallet activity of whales with more over 10,000 Eth. It demonstrates that in the final few weeks of December, the number of whale wallets increased while the number of wallets with less than ten thousand apiece decreased. This can only signify one of two things. The whales have been amassing wealth at the cost of the lesser investors. So, if you've sold all of your Eth in the last month, a whale somewhere is smiling. It's also worth noting that, in the case of both of these wallets and the Eth owned by Grayscale, the investor profile is much different than it was in 2017. Back then, the whale wallets were in the hands of wary ITO teams, and those attempting to accumulate were shrewd retail investors, both of whom had shaky hands. Neither of which saw Eth's enormous potential. This institutional accumulation was impressive through 2020, but it is simply the tip of the iceberg when it comes to institutional adoption in 2022. That's because something really spectacular was released in February. I'm referring to Ether futures. The CME listed Ether futures instruments on February 8th.

This comes after they released their first Bitcoin futures over three years ago. Although Ethereum futures have been traded on a variety of exchanges for a long time, the CME futures products are somewhat different. This is because the majority of market participants dealing in these sorts of listed products are institutions with CME broker accounts. Not your run-of-the-mill leveraged trading beginner. This, in my opinion, might herald greater institutional adoption since it provides them with another way to hedge holdings they have in the spot market. It provides them with an extra tool for portfolio optimization, and we must consider the free attention that this is expected to bring Ethereum within this C5 investment class. You can bet your bottom Eth that as soon as this is released, it will receive widespread publicity in the mainstream media. The CME will undoubtedly want to pique the curiosity of all possible clients in this wonderful new listed instrument that they have on offer. You simply need to look at what happened to Bitcoin's price when the BTC CME futures went online in late 2017. This might be the CME's opening shot in the Ethereum war. Not to mention that they debuted Bitcoin options on the exchange for the first time last year. We've seen a lot of open interest and volume since the debut of these Bitcoin options, so if the excitement for Eth futures is similar, I wouldn't be shocked if we saw Eth options on the CME by the end of the year. All of this provides not just more tools for these huge investors, but also more news articles about Ethereum's acceptance by the guys in suits. This is fantastic, but this is crypto, and everything is decentralized here. Without a question, 2020 was the year of decentralized finance, or DeFi. We started with a total value locked TVL of just under $500 million and are now at little over 28 billion. Try to wrap your mind around that. We have a 40x in the TVL, and this isn't some esoteric cryptocurrency; this is cash locked up in DeFi smart contracts. Those are some amazing figures, yet almost 95% of that DeFi is on the Ethereum blockchain. That implies that all of the cryptocurrency that has been locked over there is Ether. A total of $20 billion of Ether has been removed from the market and locked within these systems.

This is Eth that is no longer accessible on the market, implying that there is less Eth available to sell. As we all know, the economics 101 formula for price increases is less supply and greater demand. It should also be noted that this TVL is far more sticky than the monies donated to ICOs in 2017. To begin with, it is not up to ICO project teams to choose whether or not that locked Eth will be released to the market. It is entirely up to the customers who transfer their dollars there, and these people are not the same as individuals who tossed their money away in worthless ICOs in 2017. They are often more seasoned and understand why they are distributing cash. Also primarily focuses on yield optimization tactics and liquidity, but it has a favorable impact on the ecosystem. As a result of supply being locked in DeFi protocols, there is far less heat on the market. I also have some fascinating on-chain data to share with you that might assist support this storey of limited supply. This is the total quantity of Ethereum stored in exchange wallets. The quantity of Ether stored at exchanges has been steadily decreasing. Users are withdrawing Eth from exchange wallets and storing it in their own wallets. This might imply that the Eth will be pooled for investment reasons and assigned to a DeFi protocol, or that it would be delivered to the beacon chain contract. On the open market, ETH is becoming a much scarcer asset. However, this just addresses the supply side of the problem. We must not forget that Ether is also a utility currency, and you must pay fees in gas to utilize the Ethereum blockchain. All of this suggests that there will be increased demand. How is this demand shaping up? We merely need to look at the total number of transactions on the Ethereum blockchain over the last year to see this.

The number of transactions has continually increased, and it has just surpassed 1 million per day. We've observed a significant rise in the quantity of fees paid in the first few days of January. Because these gas fees are paid in Eth, the increasing demand for Eth to settle transactions leads to an increase in demand for Eth itself. What's causing all of this transactional activity? There are a variety of use cases, but many of them include stable currency. Ethereum has emerged as the primary settlement layer for the majority of stable currency transactions. We're discussing Pacs, USDC, SUSD, and last but not least tethers USDT. Over the last several months, not only has the total quantity of stablecoin created on the Ethereum network increased dramatically but so has the overall transfer volume. On the Ethereum network, billions of dollars in transaction volume are cleared. All of this indicates that there will be more demand for the network and, as a result, more demand for gas. However, this is merely the beginning. In the following months, we may expect a flood of stable currency issuance and demand on the Ethereum network. What motivates me to say that? Well, two things. First, Visa has announced a partnership with the Circle Consortium to connect Visa's worldwide payments network to USDC. To give you a sense of size, Visa's payment network includes over 60 million businesses, and the company processes trillions of dollars each year.

This means that even if only a tiny percentage of these shops begin accepting USDC payments, we are talking about billions of transactions and consistent coin demand. Given that Eth is now the largest USDC settlement layer, this all adds up to tremendous sums of utility demand right there. However, there is something else that may be more groundbreaking than the Visa collaboration. One that is likely to entrench stable coins deep throughout the US financial system. Of course, I'm referring to the Office of the Controller of the Currency's (OCC) recent stablecoin statement. The OCC has basically said that federally chartered banks can allow stablecoin payments. The OCC also stated that they will be allowed to host their own independent nodes on the stablecoin network. All of this means that banks may utilize public blockchains to confirm store records and settle payment transactions as long as they follow existing rules. To grasp the relevance of this for crypto, consider that interbank transfers are the lifeblood of business in the United States, and being able to settle these transactions on chain allows banks to accomplish them faster and more efficiently than traditional transfer methods.

The value of interbank transactions in the United States is in the trillions of dollars, and as we all know, banks are constantly looking for ways to save money while stiffing consumers. I wouldn't be shocked if a substantial percentage of early adopters chose to settle transactions like manner, and if they do, what network do you believe they'll use? That's it: tremendous utility demand for a rare asset with a restricted supply that's being rapidly added to an institutional investor portfolio. Well, there is one very important issue that I have neglected to address. On December 1st, 2020, the first phase of Ethereum 2.0 was officially launched. This was the formal debut of the beacon chain, with the Ethereum 2.0 staking contract guaranteeing sufficient cash. The importance of Eth 2.0 for the network cannot be emphasized. I can't go into all of the updates here since there are so many. The fact that a significant quantity of Ether has been trapped into the Eth 2.0 staking contract is the biggest direct consequence of Ethereum 2.0 right now. This graph displays the total amount of Eth transferred since November of 2020. We presently have more over 3 million health tied into that staking contract. Staking incentives are available to people who have deposited Eth to the staking contract. However, here's the key point: funds submitted to the deposit address cannot yet be withdrawn. This essentially indicates that the Eth locked in that deposit contract will be off the market for a while. Any further Ether descent is instantly removed from circulation. Because there is less circulating supply on the market, an asset that was originally rare has become increasingly scarcer. Let us now add all of this to the existing state of Ethereum. Increased institutional demand, increased whale demand, decreased exchange balances, increased Eth locked in DeFi, increased stable coin demand, increased Eth locked in the beacon chain What does that smell like to you? You are correct; it requires one additional element, which is EIP-1559.

This is a tasty Ethereum enhancement proposal that would alter the way the Ethereum transaction market operates. Essentially, it would modify Ethereum's present bid-based transaction market for a fixed charge; the base fee. This basic fee would then be burnt on the network, which would deplete the quantity of Eth. This might imply that the fee burn is sufficient to balance the consequences of more Eth protocol inflation. In other words, in the long term, there will be no new Eth entering the market and just the present supply. This might be fresh to the argument of many who refer to Eth's lack of a supply cap as a reason why it can't have long-term value, and it's going to be introduced, according to an Ethereum core developer. Some miners may be dissatisfied, but the majority of the community supports it. Furthermore, the miner's dissatisfaction with the update may be rendered irrelevant if Ethereum moves to proof of stake with the 2.0 upgrades. Fee burns have been added to the potion, and it is now ready for ingestion. I hope you're prepared for an exciting ride. Just a few last remarks; the Ethereum network is at a critical point in its illustrious history. It is undergoing a massive overhaul at the same time as demand is skyrocketing and supply is becoming constrained. These are all price positive, which is why prices appear to be rising. We're in the midst of a new frenzy, fueled by institutional demand from deep-pocketed whales and funds.

It is being utilized to construct a new financial paradigm, the repercussions of which will be felt for years to come. Are there any dangers? Without a doubt. There are always some. We are all aware that Eth 2.0 may be postponed. We are aware of the possibility of a significant failure in Eth 2.0, no matter how little. Those DeFi degens may opt to withdraw all of their Eth from DeFi protocols and sell it on the open market, but the dangers are quite low. Assuming that the market does really turn into a waltz, a $2,000 price is readily achievable by the middle of 2022. That is my non-financial advisor's view. You must reach your own decision.

CHAPTER 3:

HOW TO MAXIMISE YOUR PROFITS IN THE BULL RUN

This bitcoin bull market has the ability to alter people's lives for the better. There's only one minor issue: many people who are now involved in cryptocurrency have no understanding of what they're getting themselves into. As a survivor of the 2017 bull market, I can attest to having earned my fair share of purple hearts. Should I have been more prepared? So, I've learned my lesson, and this time I'm not going to let those cryptocurrency profits pass me by. So, in this chapter, I'll share my knowledge with you so that you know exactly what to expect from this bull market and how to capitalize on it. If you've been investing in cryptocurrency for longer than a month, you're probably feeling pretty good right now. Bitcoin is up more than 50%, Ethereum has more than doubled in value, and nearly every other cryptocurrency has enjoyed equal gains.

You've probably also seen a number of minor corrections, but you've recognized that these are normal given how volatile cryptocurrency is. A 10% decrease never injured anyone, but what if I told you that things are about to become far more unpredictable than you could have ever imagined? When this bull market reaches its apex, the triple-digit gains that took you months to achieve will begin to occur on a daily or even hourly basis, and the shakeouts will be just as hot. This is what happened in 2017, and I'm fairly certain it will happen again in 2022 or 2022. This is due to the fact that there will most certainly be a scarcity of cryptocurrencies on exchanges. When there isn't enough Eth on an exchange to go around, the little supply relative to the enormous demand produces incredible price fluctuation, generally to the upside. OTC traders will almost certainly aggravate this volatility. The majority of large investors purchase their cryptocurrency OTC, or over-the-counter.

This is to ensure that they do not disrupt the market or drive up prices on cryptocurrency exchanges; however, if OTC reserves run out, using an exchange will be the only viable option, which will work wonders for the price of whatever crypto they're buying, until the whales and weak hands start to sell, at which point the price will crash just as hard. You must psychologically prepare for this irrational price fluctuation. Another thing to be prepared for is an incredible amount of fud and fomo from personalities and news sites both inside and outside of the crypto world. You could think we've arrived, but believe me when I say we're only getting started. Bitcoin and cryptocurrency search patterns on Google are still far from their all-time highs. When public interest in cryptocurrencies grows, you can expect that every attention-hungry media source and inexperienced scholar will be milking the heck out of it to achieve their five seconds of glory. The worst part is that every now and then something comes out that you really should be aware of. This implies you must be able to read through these clickbait headlines objectively.

The more you understand about cryptocurrency, the easier it will be to do so. For example, if you read an ivy league professor with a triple Ph.D. in sexual socialism who believes Bitcoin is a capitalist swindle, you're probably alright. However, if you read an update from the SEC stating that one of the cryptos you're holding is a security and that the SEC is initiating legal action against the entity producing it, I believe you should immediately exit that position, no questions asked. Allow notifications from the SEC and other US regulators on Twitter so you can be the first to know. In short, you must be able to distinguish between reality and fiction and be willing and able to adjust your exit plan if the facts indicate that this is the best course of action. If you do not currently have an exit strategy, I recommend that you develop one as soon as possible. Once you've decided on your exit strategy, you should spend some time learning about technical analysis and a few basic indications. This is due to the fact that when the actual gains and losses begin to roll in, the crypto market will be driven only by emotion.

Technical analysis happens to be the old skill of detecting emotional patterns in price behavior. For hundreds of years, these patterns have replicated themselves throughout every speculative market. Because of investor psychology, bitcoin has a four-year cycle. This is why Bitcoin tends to rebound when it falls below a thousand, such as 33K or 34K, and why altcoins surge if Bitcoin trades sideways for too long. Knowing technical analysis can help you make better judgments on the fly when it comes time to sell your cryptos. In an ideal world, being psychologically and technically prepared would be sufficient to manage the bull market. Regrettably, you are not the only factor in this equation. Most of us trade on centralized cryptocurrency exchanges, and we've all seen what happens when market volatility occurs. When the markets heat up, the world's top exchanges continue to experience interruptions. Some might argue that it is done on purpose, and I believe it is a very possible possibility.

To make matters worse, when network traffic is high, it might take a very lengthy time to transfer cash, especially if you're dealing with a cryptocurrency that is susceptible to bloat. All blockchains are vulnerable, however, Bitcoin and Ethereum are frequently used as examples. You must plan ahead of time for exchange outages and transfer periods, or you may find yourself yelling at your phone or computer for hours on end while the market crashes before your eyes. You have a few possibilities in terms of solutions. The first step is to investigate joining a different cryptocurrency exchange that supports the coins you intend to sell. Just make sure the exchange is legitimate and that you won't be taken advantage of by withdrawal fees or deposit and withdrawal minimums. If you're trading Ethereum assets, using a DEX like Uni-swap may be worth the increased gas fees if it means being able to sell your tokens in minutes rather than hours.

The second alternative is to send the cryptocurrency you intend to sell to an exchange in the days or weeks preceding the sale. Keep in mind that storing big sums of bitcoin on an exchange is incredibly dangerous, and even if they have insurance, it might be years before you see those assets if something goes wrong. Finally, ensure that all of your bitcoin wallets are current. This includes maintaining software on hardware wallets like Trezor or Ledger up to current. If you haven't plugged in yours in a while, you should do it sooner rather than later. At the height of a bull market, the last thing you need is a technical issue on your end that might have been easily prevented. The true worst scenario in a bull market is being unable to payout. As you may have seen, the transition from fiat to crypto is significantly simpler than the converse. If you haven't already attempted cashing out your cryptocurrency, I strongly advise you to do so as soon as possible. My advice is to wire the monies straight to your bank account using a well-regulated cryptocurrency exchange such as Coinbase or Bitstamp. If you don't anticipate to generate a lot of money and want to use it for some of your everyday costs, you may buy a cryptocurrency debit card from a firm like Crypto.com and fill it with fiat using crypto in their app.

The exchange rates on bitcoin debit cards are generally rather excellent, and I won't deny that the cashback benefits are fantastic. Most crypto debit cards also allow you to withdraw actual currency, which is very convenient. Whichever solution you choose, be sure to test it thoroughly ahead of time and consider having backup crypto to fiat gateways in case something goes wrong. If you're unable to cash out for any reason, I highly advise transferring your assets to a transparent and well-regulated stablecoin like USDC and transferring those funds to your own wallet until you've found a means to pay out, if that's your goal. Just keep in mind that Circle, the business that provides USDC, has the authority to freeze your account if you participate in any questionable activity. You may also wish to postpone cashing out your cryptocurrency for tax concerns. If you store your cryptocurrency for more than a year in some countries, such as the United States, you will pay less tax. In crypto tax havens such as Germany, you pay no tax, and in certain situations, you may minimize your tax burden by realizing some of your gains in one tax year and waiting until the following to cash out the remainder. In many circumstances, you may lower your crypto tax burden by deducting any cryptocurrency purchases as a business cost. It may even be feasible to avoid paying any taxes at all by exploiting loopholes in gift-giving rules. Even if you decide to cash out your crypto, you should consider long and hard about what you will do with the money. There's no lack of Lambo jokes in crypto, but the true joke is spending your money on one. This is due to the fact that an automobile is a depreciating asset, and the instant you drive it off the lot, it loses up to 20% of its value. Poor investments like this are the main reason why most lottery winners go bankrupt.

They revert to the same middle-class attitude that kept them from becoming wealthy in the first place. If you've managed to go to the moon with your crypto investments, it's critical that you don't spend your way back down. Instead, consider how you may utilize that money to produce more money. Real estate appears to be a popular alternative these days, which I define as renting out a house with a large profit margin. On that point, don't be too hard on yourself if you miss the peak of this bull market or sell too soon. Selling the peak is a superhuman achievement while purchasing the drop is like catching a falling knife. Instead of wondering what if, compare your gains to those of your no coiner pals who have invested in the stock market or, worse, government bonds. The annual return on the stock market is 10% on average. You shouldn't be wailing in a corner about how your 20x return could have been a 22x. That kind of attitude might lead to you making a potentially stupid move, such as re-entering the market when you realize that the cryptos you sold are still rising in value. To be honest, there are certain circumstances where you should consider returning, and if you do your technical analysis homework, you'll be able to spot one of these excellent possibilities. Do not, under any circumstances, throw yourself into debt. Spend only what you have. However, if you still have Ethereum-based crypto assets in circulation that you might use as collateral, you may employ decentralized borrowing and lending protocols like Aave to offer yourself some more leverage.

This would allow you to withdraw a stablecoin such as USDC and buy that one cryptocurrency that simply keeps going up in value. While this is still a risk, at least you will not be in debt if things go wrong. When you've finally made it big, you have to resist the impulse to show off to the detractors. I understand that being modest is difficult in these circumstances, but the last thing you want is to bring unwanted attention to yourself. It will affect how your friends and family approach you, and it may put you at risk of being stabbed by a suspicious stranger. If life has taught me anything, it is that money comes and goes, and you don't get to keep it when the lights go out. If you fumble the ball and make nothing during this bull market, you'll still be a winner as long as you're not in debt. Why? Because you'd have obtained the knowledge you'd need to be successful in the following bull market. Perhaps you even learned a thing or two about cryptocurrency and gained a few new friends along the way. If, on the other hand, everything fell apart because you lost access to your wallet and forgot the wallet seed, that's your fault. Don't be that person. It's fantastic if you've already earned some spectacular gains during this bull run.

Still, I hope you're prepared for what's to come because it's going to be quite difficult to keep that crypto tension under control. When your portfolio fluctuates by tens of thousands of dollars each hour, it's a completely new ballgame. Eth reserves on exchanges are already depleting, and I expect other cryptocurrencies to follow suit shortly. I'm also looking forward to all of the experts that will come in and teach us the benefits and drawbacks of Bitcoin. Unless such critique comes from someone in a position to influence the market, I'll keep my ears firmly sealed to all fud and fomo. If you want to profit from an emotional market, you need to be familiar with ta and remember that there is no such thing as too much practice.

A few minutes each day of charting may represent the difference between a 10x and a 30x return. When the crypto market actually takes off, time will be of the essence. During the wild moments of late 2017, I lost thousands of dollars while waiting for my Bitcoin to be confirmed on the network. When you believe the data cell is just around the corner, you should also strive to get your coin as close to where you want it to go as possible. When it comes to selling, you must be completely confident that you have more than one exit out of the cryptocurrency market. That was one of my biggest regrets from the previous bull market, but there weren't nearly as many alternatives back then as there are now. It shouldn't be difficult to discover a trustworthy crypto-to-fiat gateway, and the sooner you get started, the better. I despise taxes as much as the next man, but I'd rather pay a few thousand dollars than lose a few years of my life. So be it if that reduces my 20x gain to a 19x game. Fortunately, there are several legal ways to lower your crypto tax. Cryptocurrency is, in my opinion, one of the finest investments you can make. I truly believe it is the future, and that is worth more than any Lambo. As a result, I'm likely to keep a sizable portion of my portfolio through this bull market as well. What I do know is that I will do my best to remain modest. After all, money isn't everything, and without my friends and family, it would all be meaningless.

CHAPTER 4:

HOW TO INVEST IN CRYPTO SAFELY

Do you want to dip your toes into the cryptocurrency markets and purchase your first coin? In this chapter, I'll walk you through my comprehensive beginner's approach to buying cryptocurrencies securely. I'll walk you through all of the processes without any of the technical jargon. All of this is to ensure that you acquire cryptocurrency correctly and safely keep your money. Before I begin, there are certain cold hard crypto realities I must disclose with you. Things to consider when purchasing a cryptocurrency. The mainstream media has recently gone crazy with Bitcoin. Bitcoin has been breaking all-time highs in headline after headline. Not only that, but they often post mind-boggling price forecasts, such as those from JP Morgan. With that kind of publicity, you might be forgiven for believing that you can just sit back, relax, take a bath, purchase crypto and watch the money pour in. Well, cryptocurrency may be a bit like the wild west at times, with hackers, frauds, and questionable exchanges aplenty. So, if you want to enter the crypto markets, you better have your six shooter ready and be ready to beat off the criminals. Furthermore, if you store bitcoin safely, you will practically have your own Swiss bank account; however, where cryptocurrency differs is that there are no transaction reversals. If something goes wrong, there is no one to call.

There is no insurance on this little Swiss bank account, which means that if your bitcoin is stolen, the government would not compensate you. Another thing I've seen my pals do is brag about how much money they've gained in these cryptocurrency marketplaces. I get how seeing your money quadruple in a matter of days might be thrilling, but who else is overhearing that conversation? There are evil individuals out there, and they may have overheard that you had tens of thousands of dollars in cryptocurrency, which is a recipe for disaster. So, if you're thinking about getting into crypto, I'd advise you to keep it to yourself. Seriously, the fewer people who know you own cryptocurrency, the better. My second piece of advice is to never spend more than you are willing to lose. Nothing in life is certain, and the same is true with cryptocurrency. If you're thinking about maxing up your credit card or spending your rent money on cryptocurrency, please don't. I should also point out that cryptocurrency is far more volatile than the stock market. If the stock market loses 7%, a circuit breaker is tripped, and trade is halted for a short period of time. A 7% drop is virtually certain to make the news, but in crypto, it's simply another day at the job. I've seen days when my whole portfolio swung up or down by more than 30%. If that's too much for you, then cryptocurrency isn't for you. I can tell you firsthand that those fluctuations cause a great deal of stress.

Another piece of advice I have for you is to be cautious about the websites you visit. There are a plethora of fraudulent websites out there posing as cryptocurrency exchanges and wallets. Those bogus websites exist to steal your login and passwords, allowing the crypto thief to make off with your cryptocurrency like a bandit, so pay attention to the precise URL of that crypto site and make sure you notice the small padlock at the upper left corner of the URL. When you see it, you know the site has an SSL certificate, which guarantees your password submission is safe. Once you've determined that you've arrived at the correct crypto website, it's a good idea to save it and use that bookmark to return to it in the future. Finally, one of the most crucial factors that perplex crypto novices are the fluctuation of cryptocurrency values. You have no idea how many times I've heard new crypto acquaintances remark, "Bitcoin is pricey; I'm going to purchase this altcoin - it's just a dollar." Because it's less expensive, and if it reaches the same price as Bitcoin, I'll be a millionaire." So here's the deal. The price of a cryptocurrency isn't the best method to judge its worth. Instead, you should be more concerned with its market capitalization. In a nutshell, the market cap is just the quantity of coins circulating for that cryptocurrency multiplied by its price. It offers you a much better understanding of how cryptocurrencies are valued in relation to one another. Coingecko.com and coinmarketcap.com are two sites I recommend for doing so.

The important to remember here is that just because a cryptocurrency is priced at a few cents per coin doesn't imply it's cheap or that you're getting a good deal, so keep that in mind. Do you still want to participate in the crypto markets now that you've learned these unpleasant crypto truths? If this is the case, there are a few things you should do to prepare.

I should tell out that there is nothing keeping you from purchasing that cryptocurrency right now, but remember how I mentioned all those hackers and robbers out there attempting to steal people's cryptocurrency? So, before we acquire Fort Knox, we need to build our own version of it. Would you honestly expect a bar of gold to remain there after 30 minutes if you purchased it and put it on the street? Obviously not. So I'm going to explain five actions you can do to assist guarantee that you can safely keep your cryptocurrency. First, get yourself a pen and a piece of paper. Simply said, if you write down all of your crypto logins, passwords, and seed phrases on paper, it cannot be hacked by some random computer whiz on the other side of the world. I don't intend to seem paranoid, but making duplicates of this sensitive material and storing them in multiple locations might be a smart idea. One duplicate, for example, can be hidden in your sock drawer and another in a safe deposit box across town. As a result, if your house burns down, you won't lose access to your cryptocurrency. Another technique for carefully saving these crucial facts is to place them in sealed ziploc bags. That way, even if your house has a leak, your crypto passwords should be protected. Finally, you might wish to guard against a home guest or maid accidentally discovering the keys to your crypto riches.

To do this, you may wish to conceal certain characteristics by purchasing a UV pen and a black light. This makes the piece of paper appear to be blank. As a result, practically anyone who discovers the keys to your crypto kingdom will have no idea what they're looking at. Step two is to understand that hackers are not like that kid at school who guessed your laptop's password.

Password guessing by hand is a thing of the past. Instead, they utilize a brute force attack, in which they throw a database of passwords at your account in the hope that one of them works. So, how can you defend against brutes on the other side of the world attempting to brute force your accounts? Having very lengthy passwords with digits, capital letters, and special characters, on the other hand, dramatically increases the number of combinations that a bot must try in order to accurately guess your password.

With the password cracking tools that are now available, that hacker may have to wait hundreds of years before being able to guess that strong password. But how do you step up your password security game? I would propose that you use a separate password for each crypto account.

That implies that if someone obtains one, they will be unable to access the others. Some individuals also want to save time by utilizing password managers, but these are problematic since if hackers gain access, they will have the keys to your crypto kingdom. Back in 2017, a crypto YouTuber had his Evernote account stolen while live streaming, causing his cryptocurrency to spill out. The next step is to ensure that your computer is free of any malicious viruses or key loggers. Perhaps you followed a link on a dubious website in the past, and your machine has been infected with a key logger. If this occurs, a hacker will be able to obtain all of your passwords as you input them on your keyboard. You may use a free virus scanner like Malwarebytes to discover if there is anything malicious on your computer. Install it and conduct a virus check to ensure that everything is in order behind the hood.

The fourth step is to ensure that your phone is safe. After that, you'll want to use two-factor authentication to secure all of your exchange accounts. Using SMS-based two-factor authentication is a common rookie error. This is really highly dangerous owing to a sim-swap assault. This is when a criminal contacts your cell provider and persuades them to port your number to their phone. After that, they can obtain your two-factor pin and reset your passwords. Millions of dollars in the cryptocurrency have been taken from users as a result of these types of assaults. So, what's the answer? Install an authenticator app, which produces one-time pins locally on the smartphone. It essentially connects to the exchange server and cannot be surpassed. This is done by a variety of programs, including Google authenticator, Authy, and Microsoft's authenticator.

Every 30 seconds, they create a new six-digit code that must be entered into a computer in order to access your exchange account. My sixth recommendation is that you create a separate email account that you will exclusively use for crypto-related matters. After all, you've most likely been using the same email address since you were 12 years old, right? That indicates there are likely thousands of people who are aware of it. Proton Mail is my personal preference. They're encrypted and thus far more safe than ordinary email service providers, so go to protonmail.com and set up a new email account only for crypto exchanges or wallets.

The advantage of using a new email address is that it makes it more difficult for anybody to gain access to your crypto accounts if they are able to hack your personal email. You also have the option of separating your personal emails from crypto-related ones. In the Proton Mail account, do not use your entire name or surname. It removes one more clue that hackers may use to identify you. Once you've gotten all of that protection in place, you'll need a wallet to properly store your cryptocurrency. I understand that there are many really secure exchanges available and that you may be concerned about storing your bitcoin on your own. But you must understand that crypto stored on an exchange is nothing more than an IOU. You don't have the keys, and if the transaction is ever compromised, you might be left holding the bag. That is why, if you are going to be holding a significant quantity of cryptocurrency, I would advise you to self-custody it and keep it in an offline wallet. Even better, you should acquire yourself a hardware wallet. These hardware wallets range in price from sixty to one hundred and eighty dollars, but for the finest crypto security money can buy, it appears to be a more than acceptable price. When you set up your hardware wallet, you'll be given 24 seed words.

You should definitely jot things down on that critical piece of paper I mentioned before. Essentially, if you lose or damage your device, you may use the seed words on a new hardware wallet to restore access to your cryptocurrency. Those seed words will work with any BIP 39 equipped crypto wallet, allowing you to access your cash even if Tresor or Ledger go out of business. In summary, if you're going to spend a few thousand dollars in the cryptocurrency markets, having a hardware wallet is definitely the greatest move you can make. That's a little thing to pay for peace of mind. If you performed all of the processes correctly, you should now have that piece of paper with all of your critical crypto information on it. You've set up your crypto email, you've got your crypto wallet, and you've protected your computer and phone. So you've taken all of the necessary security steps and are now ready for the next step, which is to purchase that cryptocurrency.

The ideal approach to acquire cryptocurrency for you will depend on a number of factors, including your location, the individual cryptocurrencies you wish to purchase, and the payment method you want. However, if you live in Europe or nations such as the United Kingdom, Canada, Singapore, or Switzerland, the Swissborg app is the simplest option I've discovered to buy cryptocurrency using a bank account. The bad news for anyone based in the United States is that Swissborg cannot be used. Swissborg allows you to purchase common cryptocurrencies like Bitcoin and Ethereum, as well as a few more unusual cryptocurrencies such as Engine currency. So, how do you get that cryptocurrency? So, click the download app button to go to the app store. Install and launch the app on your phone. On the home screen, there is a large "get started" button. When you click that, you'll be prompted to provide your phone number. Following that, you'll receive an SMS message with a six-digit number. Put that in there. Secure and authenticate your Swissborg app with a four-digit pin. Then you must agree to Swissborg's terms of service and privacy policies. To agree, move the slider to the right and press the next button.

Then you'll be prompted to provide your name, birth date, and nationality. You will then be prompted to provide your email address. Then you'll need to confirm your email address. To access your inbox, click the mail icon. Once you've pressed the verify email address button, you'll see a green tick indicating that your email address has been validated, and you'll need to click the open Swissborg app button to log back in. When you return to the app, you'll need to enter your postcode to discover your address. You may also manually input your address. You will next be asked about your investment experience, job status, occupation, and source of cash. Then it's time to authenticate yourself. To get started, click the next button. You'll then be instructed to locate an ID document and prepare to snap a selfie. Choose the identification document you want to submit for verification. The next step is to grant Swissborg access to your camera. To enable the camera button, press that.

Then just snap a photo of your passport or other identification paper and shoot a selfie. When you have it, you are ready to make a deposit with Swissborg. To do so, go to Portfolio and press the Deposit button. Your country's native currency will be displayed here, so select it. Finally, you'll discover Swissborg's banking information. Log in to your online banking and make a payment using your Swissborg credentials. The most important thing to remember is to provide the random reference number in your transaction so that your deposit may be linked to your Swissborg account. Once you've made your payment from your bank account, you can sit back and rest while you wait for the funds to arrive in your Swissborg account. When the deposit is completed, you will be able to purchase your cryptocurrency. In the app, go to the marketplace and choose the cryptocurrency you wish to buy. You might, for example, choose Bitcoin. The next step is to decide from which balance you wish to purchase the Bitcoin. You'll want to click that because you've deposited fiat money.

Then just enter the quantity of Bitcoin you wish to purchase and press the next button. Finally, you'll be given a final cost. Simply confirm your purchase, and you've purchased that cryptocurrency. It's also worth noting that this procedure is essentially the same for purchasing any cryptocurrency supported by Swissborg. You'll want to withdraw that cryptocurrency to your hardware wallet now that you've purchased it to keep it safe. To do so, go to your portfolio and click on the cryptocurrency you want to withdraw. A send button can be found in the bottom right corner of the screen. Finally, you'll see a field where you can enter the address you got from your hardware wallet. Copy and paste it, double-check that it is correct, and then click Next to send that cryptocurrency to your hardware wallet. Of course, you can also send that Bitcoin or Ethereum to another exchange and trade it for more exotic altcoins. Purchasing cryptocurrency on Swissborg is truly that simple. But where is the best place to buy cryptocurrency if you live in the United States? Binance US and Coinbase Pro are the two most popular options.

Both of those options will require you to secure your account with 2FA, so it's a good thing you already have that sorted. You've probably heard about a hot new altcoin that you'd like to get your hands on. Assume you want to buy injective protocol and are unsure which exchange you can do so on. You can find out by visiting Coingecko or Coinmarketcap and searching for that hot altcoin. After that, you'll be taken to the cryptocurrency information page. When you click the markets button, it will display all of the different exchanges where it is listed. Then you can see that you'll probably want to open a Binance account to buy INJ. You can use this method to determine which other exchanges exist. To get that exotic cryptocurrency you've been eyeing, you'll need to open an account. If you want my opinion, I find the majority of the coins I'm looking for on Binance. When compared to Swissborg, it also accepts regular fiat deposits, but there are a few more steps involved in getting your fiat sent here. If you want to buy those exotic altcoins, you'll need a Binance account in either case. That concludes my ultimate beginner's guide to purchasing cryptocurrency. I know there was a lot to take in there, and I may have scared you away from investing in cryptocurrency, but I believe it's best, to be honest about how things are. People can then decide for themselves whether or not all of this is for them. There are many other great ways to buy cryptocurrency, but we wanted to share the ones that are the quickest and easiest with you.

CHAPTER 5:

HOW TO INVEST AND TRADE CARDANO & POLKADOT

The year 2022 will be the year of smart contract blockchains. Not counting Tether half of the top 10 cryptocurrencies by market cap are smart contract compatible and these projects are all seeking the current leader; Ethereum. There are two large-cap smart contract cryptos that stand out as the most likely heirs to the throne. Of course, I'm referring to Cardano and Polkadot. These two have seen unprecedented amounts of development and adoption in the last year, and as a result, they are neck and neck in the market cap rankings. Polkadot and Cardano are also about to release major updates to their networks. This has many wondering which of the two projects will triumph as the true alternative to Ethereum in 2022. So in this chapter, I will be comparing Cardano and Polkadot and reveal which one has the best chance of becoming the next hotbed for smart contracts and decentralized cryptocurrency applications.

When it comes to comparing cryptocurrency projects there are a lot of different metrics you can use. Given the size and complexity of both Cardano and Polkadot, I'm not going to get super technical. Instead, I'm going to stick to metrics that everyone can understand, starting with the least technical metric of all; comparing the founders of both projects. Dr. Gavin Wood is the founder of Polkadot. He's a computer scientist and holds a Ph.D. in human computer interfacing. Gavin is also the founder of the Web3 foundation, a Swiss non-profit which oversees the development of Polkadot, and is the founder of Parity technologies which is a for-profit software development company based in the UK. It is commissioned by the Web3 foundation to develop and maintain Polkadot. Charles Hoskinson is the founder of Cardano. He is a mathematician but does not have a Ph.D. Charles is also the founder of Input Output Hong Kong or IOHK for short, which is a for-profit software development company based in Hong Kong. IOHK and a Japanese for-profit software development company called Emurgo are commissioned by the Cardano foundation also a Swiss non-profit to develop Cardano.

Charles does not hold any official title at the Cardano foundation, which sports five council members. By contrast, the Web3 foundation has only three council members and one of them is Gavin. Charles and Gavin also co-founded Ethereum with Vitalik Buterin and five others in 2013. Charles left Ethereum in June of 2014, 13 months before the Ethereum main net went live. This was apparently due to a disagreement between him and Vitalik about accepting venture capital funding, which Charles supported and Vitalik opposed. Gavin left Ethereum in January 2016 to deliver on the promises Ethereum could not, referring to the rollout of Ethereum 2.0, which had originally been scheduled to happen shortly after the Ethereum main net went live in 2015. Until his departure, Gavin had served as Ethereum CTO where he authored the Ethereum yellow paper, invented the solidity coding language, and even coded the first functional version of Ethereum. Though both Gavin and Charles are incredibly brilliant, Charles seems to spend a lot more time engaging with the Cardano community, than Gavin does with the Polkadot community.

More importantly, Gavin and Charles have radically different approaches to building their respective projects and this is a reflection of their own individual personalities. Everything that ends up on Polkadot first goes through Kusama an unaudited clone of Polkadot. By contrast, everything that ends up on Cardano is peer-reviewed by some of the smartest people in the World before being tested and implemented. As far as technology goes, Cardano and Polkadot are both proof-of-stake blockchains. That said, they have notably different architectures which again seems inspired by the personalities and experiences of their founders. Given that Polkadot was invented to deliver on the promises Ethereum could not, Polkadot is strangely similar to Ethereum 2.0. Polkadot uses an elaborate hybrid consensus mechanism called Grandpa / Babe, which allows the network to process around 1,000 transactions per second.

Gavin has noted that Polkadot has a theoretical upper limit of 1 million transactions per second with power chains and multithreading. Polkadot is essentially an ecosystem of blockchains called Parachains, that are connected to Polkadot's core blockchain called the Relay chain. These power chains will host all the smart contracts and DAPps in Polkadot's ecosystem, and there will be an initial limit of 100 Parachains. Unfortunately, it's not yet clear whether these Parachains will be interoperable at the outset which is going to be a key factor in the adoption of Polkadot once these Parachains start to go live later this year. In contrast to Polkadot, Cardano has a more original design.

The Cardano blockchain has two layers; the Cardano settlement layer which keeps track of token balances and transfers, and the Cardano computation layer which runs all the smart contracts. Cardano uses a consensus mechanism called Ouroboros proof of stake, which allows the network to process a few hundred transactions per second. However, once the hydra scaling solution is implemented, Cardano will be able to process 1 000 transactions per second for every validator that's connected to the network. This means that Cardano would need 1,000 validators to match the speed of Polkadot in its final form. On that note, Cardano still has a way to go before you can call it a finished product. We are only at stage two of five in Cardano's development roadmap, with the remaining stages set to occur in the next year or two. The next stage is set to go live in March of this year and will enable smart contracts on Cardano. Staking on Cardano and Polkadot is where things really start to get interesting. Starting with Cardano, there are currently over 1500 validators that are collectively staking over 70 percent of all ADA in circulation. Delegation can be done directly from the URI and Daedalus wallets and offers a return of around 5 percent per year in ADA. Polkadot has around 300 validators that are collectively staking over 60 percent of all Dot in circulation. Nomination which is Polkadot's version of delegation can be done using the Polkadot JS browser extension and offers a return of around 14 percent per year in Dot.

You might be thinking Polkadot is the clear winner here and you'd be right were it not for one small detail. When you stake on Polkadot, that Dot has a 28 day unlocking period if and when you decide to withdraw. On Cardano, you can withdraw your ADA at any time you like. The fine print on Cardano's taking is that the first time you stake you will not earn any rewards for the first 20 days and will only be able to claim rewards after 25 days. After that initial 25 day period, you can stake and unstake as you please with no penalties. That said, staking on Cardano seems to be a bit risky as Daedalus and URI are not the most stable wallets out there, and any big updates to Cardano can lead to technical issues for delegators. Despite these issues, Cardano is technically five times more decentralized than Polkadot in terms of validators, and Cardano explicitly intends to become the most decentralized cryptocurrency blockchain in existence. By contrast, Polkadot has an upper limit of 1000 validators.

The most obvious difference between Cardano and Polkadot in this regard is the difference in their token supply. ADA has a current supply of around 31.8 billion with a maximum supply of 45 billion. Dot has a current supply of 960 million and an initial supply of 1 billion. Logically, the larger the supply the lower the value of the coin which is why Dot is worth 16 and ADA is worth 35 cents, even though both have similar market caps. You'd be surprised how often this basic economic fact flies over the head of retail investors. Dot is inflationary to the tune of about eight percent per year and this inflation is used to reward validators and nominators. That stated, one percent of each dot that was not spent from the Polkadot treasury gets burnt every month. Even while ADA is not inflationary roughly 13.9 billion ADA will progressively be coined over the next two decades to pay for staking incentives, which works out to a functional inflation rate of around seven percent each year. ADA's supply dynamics are a bit more intricate than this.

One important difference between Dot and ADA is a token allotment. Just over 80 percent of ADA's original supply of 31 billion is in the hands of the community compared to fifty percent for Dot. This is evident in the account balances of both cryptocurrencies which demonstrated that ADA's supply is more equally distributed, compared to the supply of Dot which is significantly concentrated in the top 100 wallets. Speaking about wallets, there are approximately 300 000 Cardano wallets compared to just under 110 000 Polkadot wallets. This is really fairly strong given Polkadot has been operational for less than a year, whereas Cardano has been around since September 2017.

This also provides dot an edge from a technical analysis viewpoint, as it does not have a big previous all-time high where it may face some substantial resistance. By comparison, ADA may get rejected at its prior highs of roughly 1.2 Dollars when the next altcoin cycle starts, because I'm sure there are more than a few investors who purchased the top that want to earn back their losses. As far as adoption goes, Polkadot looks to be the current frontrunner. There are approximately 350 projects building on Polkadot, 17 of which are DAP-s. As far as I can tell there is currently only one DAPp building on Cardano and that's Bondly Finance but before Dot holders laugh their way to the bank, consider this; while Polkadot still seems to be building its bridge to Ethereum, Cardano finished its ERC20 converter in the fall of 2020 and demoed it in their October update. To say that it looks spectacular is an understatement. During this demo, the IOHK team highlighted they are ready to help Ethereum projects clone or move their projects to Cardano. Many of them may easily be done, given that the ERC20 converter allows you to burn the tokens on Ethereum to generate an equivalent quantity on Cardano. Smart contract capability for Cardano is scheduled to appear as early as March of 2022 with the release of Gogen.

This will give Cardano a large head start over Polkadot, which may not see any DAPps launching on it until the end of the year. This weight might even stretch until 2022 if the Polkadot team decides to try their Parachain auctions on Kusama first, which seems to be the idea. Moreover, each DAPp on Polkadot will require its own Parachain and there are only 100 spaces available. This technically implies that Polkadot will be restricted to 100 DAPps. No such limit exists for Cardano. Before ADA holders get too thrilled, remember this. Although the quantity of DAPps on Polkadot will be restricted, the Parachain loan offering process will ensure that every single one of those DAPps is a game changer. These Parachain loan offers will also make it feasible to launch ICOs in a new fashion that looks to skirt any existing rules. Either that, or it'll place Polkadot in the sights of authorities. Given what I presented in this chapter, it's clear to understand how both Cardano and Polkadot rank among the top 10 cryptocurrencies by market cap. I just scraped the surface of what they are up to, but we have enough evidence to draw a conclusion regarding which one will become the next Ethereum. Even though, neither Charles Hoskinson nor Gavin Wood has authority over their respective initiatives, who they are and how they behave themselves, undoubtedly has an impact. Charles may not have the same qualifications that Gavin has, but Charles is cool, calculated, and very concerned with the development of Cardano.

This is a key part of why Cardano has such a huge and engaged community. Polkadot likewise has a huge community but for a totally different cause. As a pioneer of smart contract technology, Gavin appears to attract the same type of forward-thinking developers that are developing DAPps that establish communities. In my perspective, this is what has made Polkadot so successful, thus far. Despite their completely different methods of development, Cardano and Polkadot seem to be well-matched as far as specs go, and whether you choose one over the other, ultimately depends on what you value more in a crypto project. If you appreciate decentralization, then you probably choose Cardano. If you value staking rewards, then you probably favor Polkadot. If you prioritize interoperability then Cardano looks to be the winner. But, if you're on the quest for the next 100x cryptocurrency, you'll undoubtedly find it in Polkadot's huge ecosystem. Until Polkadot starts plugging in those power chains though, any troubles with Ethereum will undoubtedly send developers rushing across Cardano's ERC20 bridge seeking sanctuary. In terms of raw price potential, you might say you're better off with ADA because it has a smaller price tag which will draw investment from novice retail investors. However, you might just as well claim that Dot will perform better because of the 28 days unlock time for the hundreds of millions of Dot that are presently being staked, which reduces the market ready supply. Then then, one might contradict that allegation with the reality that most dot tokens are contained in only a few dozen wallets. Any one of those may suddenly chuck their dot and wreck the price. Overall, both projects are so evenly matched that you may as well flip a coin when selecting which will outperform the other

CHAPTER 6:

HOW TO SAVE MONEY ON ETHEREUM GAS FEES

You may be aware that Ethereum's hefty gas prices have rendered the network nearly useless. Previously, the consequences of high gas costs were primarily felt by individuals utilizing DeFi protocols and decentralized exchanges such as Uniswap, where a simple swap may cost you more than $100 in gas. Even centralized exchanges charge fees of up to $40 USD to withdraw ERC20 stable currencies like USDT and USDC. I have just heard that someone paid more than $120 in gas only to move their Aave tokens to another Ethereum wallet address. So, in this chapter, I'll describe how Ethereum gas works, how to cut gas expenses, and even how to benefit from growing gas prices. The Ethereum network, like any other cryptocurrency, includes transaction fees called as gas. Ethereum gas costs are measured in gigawei, abbreviated as Wei. Wei is the Eth cryptocurrency's lowest denomination. One Wei is one-billionth of an Eth, and one Wei is one quintillionth of an Eth. These gas costs are paid to Ethereum miners in order for your transaction to be executed. To put it another way, the transaction must be included in the next Ethereum block. The gas costs are typically believed to be set by Ethereum miners, however, this isn't exactly accurate.

Ethereum miners vote to establish the gas limit, which determines how much gas may be contained in each Ethereum block. This gas limit used to be roughly three million Wei every Ethereum block. The gas limit is now more than 12 million Wei. If you're wondering why miners would raise the gas limit, it's because it allows the Ethereum network to fit more transactions into each block. This potentially makes the Ethereum network marginally cheaper and quicker for consumers while maintaining Ethereum miners' transaction fee earnings. The concern is that increasing the gas cap raises the barrier to entry for new Ethereum miners and Ethereum nodes, endangering the Ethereum network's decentralization. Increasing the gas limit does not affect the fact that each Ethereum block has a restricted amount of transaction space. Even if you have a greater gas limit, if the Ethereum network is busy enough, you will have to pay a premium to have the Ethereum miners include your transaction in the next Ethereum block.

When the price of Eth is low, a few hundred Wei in gas costs isn't much, but when the price of Eth is pushing through new all-time highs, it may cost a few dollars. Naturally, the more complicated the transaction, the more Ethereum gas you'll have to spend to have it included in the next block. Interacting with most DeFi protocols now costs hundreds of dollars in Eth. This effectively limits Ethereum DeFi to those with large funds. That being said, there are several strategies to lower these exorbitant Ethereum gas expenses. Before sending a transaction, almost every Ethereum wallet allows you to establish your own personal gas limit. The gas limit displayed in wallets like as MyEtherwallet and Metamask differs from the gas limit set by miners in each of the Ethereum blocks I described. Your personal gas limit is effectively the most Wei you're prepared to spend for that transaction to complete. Many Ethereum wallets will provide you the choice of sending your transaction at a slow, standard, or quick pace.

The gas fees they tell you for each of these transaction speeds are frequently out of the current. That is not their fault. The quantity of gas required to complete a transaction varies from block to block. That is why, before sending an Ethereum transaction from a wallet, you should first visit a website like Eth gas station to view the most recent gas costs. You may install their browser extension plugin to keep track of your gas costs at all times. Once you've determined the real cost for the transaction you want to send, you may manually input the quantity of Wei you're ready to pay in your Ethereum wallet. If you want to take it a step further, there's a wonderful website called https://txstreet.com/ that displays you how the gas prices change from block to block in real-time. Using these tools to set your own custom gas restrictions, you may cut your Ethereum gas expenditures by up to 30%. Another comparable method is to transact during Ethereum's quiet hours.

These are between 8 and 11 p.m. UTC, and Ethereum gas costs can be up to 50% lower during that time period. Before you perform an Ethereum transaction, you should question yourself if it is truly necessary to do so right now. Unless you're performing a mind-boggling arbitrage transaction with a flash loan, adhering to the basic minimum gas limit displayed at each gas station during Ethereum's quiet hours is definitely the best way to go. Just be careful not to pump in too little gas, or your transaction may become stuck. This is far worse than it sounds since you won't be able to send any more transactions from that wallet until the blocked transaction is either pushed through with additional gas or reversed. If you opt to brute force the transaction with extra gas, you must use at least 10% more than the last charge, regardless of current gas prices. If you change your mind and wish to reverse the transaction, you must locate the unsuccessful transaction on Ether scan, navigate to the further information, and locate the transaction's nonce number. Then, using the current gas price and the nonce number as a reference, you simply transmit zero Ethereum to your own Ethereum address. This will replace the blocked transaction, thereby canceling it and allowing fresh transactions to be sent. Metamask makes it simple to accelerate or terminate stalled transactions. Gas tokens are the way to go if you want to conserve gas while earning from high gas expenses on Ethereum.

A group of blockchain experts from multiple top-tier colleges across the world created the first gas token in late 2017. Gas tokens make use of an Ethereum mechanism known as the "storage refund." This is when the Ethereum network refunds a portion of the Eth used for gas in a smart contract when some of the data contained inside it is removed. The storage refund function exists to encourage developers to free up space on the Ethereum blockchain, which contains all smart contract data. Gas tokens are simply garbage data contained within a fake smart contract that may be deleted in exchange for Ethereum gas. The primary idea behind gas tokens is to mint them when gas prices are low and then burn them to cut gas prices by 50% when gas prices are high. Gas tokens, on the other hand, may be traded for a profit on decentralized exchanges like Uniswap, and gas tokens are a significant reason why many cryptocurrency wallets that used to supply Ethereum gas or gas subsidies ceased doing so in the autumn of 2020. Users who were astute understood they could use the free Ethereum gas offered by these wallets to create gas tokens that could be sold for a tidy profit later on. Although the original gas token is unaudited and appears to have some questionable tokenomics, DEX aggregator built an upgraded version of the original gas token dubbed the "Chi gas token" in June of 2020. The Chi gas token has risen 20x since the crash and continues to climb in line with Ethereum's gas prices.

The Chi gas token may be produced using Eth on the 1-inch exchange and a maximum of 140 Chi can be coined at a time. Before you go out to fill your bags, keep in mind that minting these gas tokens, paradoxically, demands a lot of gas. To only break even on the minting, the Dollar value of Chi would have to increase by more than 50%. Fortunately, you can make limit orders on the 1 inch exchange to automatically sell that Chi when it reaches the higher price you're aiming for. If you're purchasing Chi to save money on petrol, you can utilize it on the one inch exchange or curve financing to save up to 40 percent on gas. You must use the original gas token if you need to utilize gas tokens in other DeFi protocols. The last way to save money on Ethereum gas fees is to employ a layer 2 scaling solution. Loopring is most likely the most significant example here. Loopring, in addition to being a decentralized exchange, allows you to send Eth and LRC to other users for free. However, getting your monies into Loopring does cost gas, so whether you adopt this option is entirely dependent on your final goal. Loopering is definitely your best choice if you're continually moving Ethereum-based funds to other individuals.

When Ethereum fees are cheap, you might load up your account ahead of time and then transmit those assets later with no gas. Loopring may also be useful when it comes time to sell. We've all seen how centralized exchanges encounter technical difficulties when the price of Bitcoin or Ethereum begins to fluctuate. Loopring's AMM allows you to exchange wrapped Bitcoin and Ethereum for stable currencies like USDC and USDT, and I doubt there will be any outages when the market truly starts to move. You will also not spend an arm and a leg in gas for a swap, as you would on a layer 1 DEX like Uniswap. Just keep in mind that the Loopering AMM lacks the volume of a centralized exchange. This means that you may encounter some slippage with certain trading pairs.

To conclude, I'd like to provide you with some EIP1559 updates. If you are new to Ethereum Improvement Proposal 1559, it would establish a flat cost for Ethereum transactions and then burn those fees out of circulation. The deflationary effect from those fee burning might significantly boost Ethereum's price in 2022. An Ethereum developer stated that they will be implementing EIP1559 shortly, yet it has still not been completed nearly two months later. This appears to be due to Ethereum miners' dissatisfaction with EIP1559. To say they're making a fortune off of these gas taxes is an understatement, and they're claiming that EIP1559 is a scheme to benefit speculators and investors. Given that investors like Greyscale are desperate for EIP1559 to become a reality, I can understand their reasoning. According to a recent Tweet by Ethereum developer Tim Beiko, they are currently working on EIP1559 and expect it to be "ready to be considered for mainnet sometime in March." If I'm not mistaken, there are just two stages remaining until they begin testing it. I also spotted a line item within the Community Outreach subheading that states "outreach to minors to better understand their concerns to 1559 and stance if it is to be implemented on mainnet." Let's just hope it isn't the deciding factor in Ethereum's much-needed update.

There's no doubting that Ethereum gas taxes have been excessive, and they appear to be becoming worse in the coming months. This isn't only because the network will become busier. It's also because far too many people still don't grasp how Ethereum gas works. I can't tell you how many times I set the maximum transaction fee in Ethereum wallets like Metamask while submitting a transaction when I was a crypto newbie. I'm sure there are thousands of other Ethereum users that do this for every transaction out of habit, either because they're impatient or because they don't know any better. If everyone understood how to establish the right gas limit for the sorts of transactions they're conducting, gas prices might be far lower than they are currently. While I'm a big supporter of the notion of gas tokens, I can't claim I've ever used one in a transaction.

A 50% savings on gas expenses is fantastic, but if I'm still paying a few hundred dollars for a switch after the discount, I don't understand the benefit of utilizing them. I also can't help but note that the Chi gas token appears to be pretty inflated as regular investors come in. In contrast, I believe there is a very compelling reason why layer 2s such as Loopering and XDI have been doing well in recent weeks. Even if EIP1559 is on the way, the track record of Ethereum's developers says we'll have to wait until long after March to see the sparks flare. Layer 2s will continue to gain traction till then. Also, don't expect Ethereum miners to vote against EIP1559. They may be aware that if Ethereum becomes worthless, the rich transaction fees would vanish along with the users who paid them. Furthermore, Ethereum 2.0 is gradually but steadily coming together. This renders proof-of-work mining useless, as Ethereum 2.0 employs proof-of-stake mining instead. My only question is, how long can this go on? Just remember to transfer those monies around before selling them, and to do it when the network is somewhat less clogged.

CHAPTER 7:

BITCOIN INVESTING FUNDAMENTALS

What exactly does it mean to own a Bitcoin? Many people have heard of Bitcoin, which is a purely digital currency that does not require a government to issue it or banks to handle accounts and verify transactions. Furthermore, no one knows who invented it. However, many individuals do not know the complete answer to this issue. To get there, and to ensure that the technical aspects underpinning this response feel motivated, we'll walk through how you may have developed your own version of Bitcoin step by step. We'll start by having you use a shared ledger to keep track of payments with your buddies. Then, if you lose faith in your friends and the world around you, and if you're clever enough to incorporate a few cryptographic methods to assist sidestep the requirement for trust, you end up with what's known as a cryptocurrency.

Bitcoin was only the first cryptocurrency to be introduced, and there are currently many more on exchanges with regular currencies. Walking the road of designing your own can help establish the groundwork for understanding some of the game's more recent players and seeing where there's space for new design options. In fact, one of the reasons I picked this topic is because of the enormous surge in interest, investment, and publicity focused on digital currencies in the previous several years. We should all agree that anyone intending to purchase a cryptocurrency should thoroughly understand what it is. Not just in terms of parallels with hazy links to gold mining, but also in terms of what computers perform when transmitting, receiving, and producing cryptocurrency. One point to emphasize is that, while you will go into the underlying technicalities, you do not need to know those specifics to utilize a cryptocurrency. You don't need to know the specifics of what occurs behind the scenes when you swipe a credit card.

There are a plethora of user-friendly programs that allow you to send and receive these currencies as effortlessly as any other digital payment.

The distinction is that the fundamental backbone is not a bank validating transactions, but rather a sophisticated method of decentralized trustless verification based on some of the math created in cryptography. To begin, lay aside the idea of cryptocurrency for a few moments. We'll begin the narrative with something more mundane: Digital signatures and ledgers It might be inconvenient to swap cash all the time if you and your pals exchange money regularly, such as paying your half of the dinner bill. As an example, you may keep a shared ledger that records payments that you want to make in the future. Alice pays Bob $20, Bob pays Charlie $40, and so forth.

This ledger will be public and open to the public, similar to a website where anybody can go and simply enter new lines. You all go over the list of transactions at the end of each month and total everything up. If you spent more than you received, you put that money back into the pot; if you received more than you spent, you take that amount out. The process for becoming a part of this system is as follows: Anyone may add lines to the ledger, and everyone gets together at the end of each month to settle up with real money. One issue with a public ledger like this is that anybody may add a line, so what's to stop Bob from coming in and writing "Alice gives Bob $100" without Alice's approval? How can we be sure that all of these transactions are what the sender intended?

This is when the first bit of encryption enters the picture: Signatures in digital form. The idea here is that, similar to a handwritten signature, Alice should be able to put anything next to a transaction that demonstrates she has viewed it and approved of it. And no one else should be able to fake her signature. At first
57

glance, it may appear that digital signatures aren't even conceivable, because whatever data makes up the signature may be read and reproduced by any machine, so how can you avoid forgeries? The way this works is that everyone produces a public key/private key pair, which looks like a string of bits. Because the private key is also known as the secret key, we may shorten it to SK while abbreviating the public key to PK. The secret key, as the titles imply, is something you should keep to yourself. In the real world, no matter what document you're signing, your handwritten signature appears the same. Because it varies for various communications, a digital signature is significantly more powerful. It seems to be a string of 1's and 0's, typically around 256 bits, and even little modifications to the message entirely affect what your signature on that message should look like. Formally, creating a signature entails some function that is dependent on both the message and your private key.

The private key ensures that the signature can only be produced by you, and the fact that it is dependent on the message means that no one can just duplicate one of your signatures and forge it on another message. This is accompanied by a function to check the validity of a signature, which is where the public key comes into play. It just outputs true or false to indicate if this was a signature generated by the private key associated with the public key used for verification. I won't get into specifics of how these functions operate, but the idea is that if you don't know the secret key, it should be impossible to find a valid signature. There is no better technique than simply guessing and testing if random signatures are valid using the public key until you find one that works. With 256 bits, there are 2256 potential signatures, and you must discover one that works. This is an absurdly huge number. To term it astronomically enormous would be giving astronomy too much credit.

Let's just state that when you verify a signature against a particular message and public key, you can be certain that the only way someone could have made it was if they had the secret key linked with the public key. There is one little issue here: If Alice signs a transaction such as "Alice pays Bob $100," even if Bob cannot counterfeit Alice's signature on new messages, he may simply replicate that same line as many times as he likes since the message/signature combination is legal. To get around this, we require that when you sign a transaction, the message include a unique ID connected with that transaction. As a result, if Alice gives Bob $100 numerous times, each transaction necessitates a new signature. Digital signatures eliminate a significant component of confidence from our first protocol. Even yet, this is based on a type of honor system.

Specifically, you're assuming that everyone will follow through and settle up in cash at the end of each month. But what if Charlie, for example, has amassed thousands of dollars in debt and simply refuses to show up? If some individuals owe a lot of money, the only true incentive to resort to cash to settle things is if they owe a lot of money. So maybe you have the brilliant notion that you never have to settle up in cash as long as you have some means to keep individuals from spending more than they bring in.

Start by having everyone put $100 into the pot, and have the first few lines of the ledger say "Alice receives $100, Bob gets $100, and so on." Simply refuse transactions when someone spends more than they have on the ledger. For example, if the first two transactions are "Charlie pays Alice $50" and "Charlie pays Bob $50," attempting to add "Charlie pays you $20" would be invalid, the same as if he had never signed it. This implies that you must be aware of the entire history of transactions in order to verify if a new one is genuine. This is likely to be true for cryptocurrencies as well, albeit there is still space for improvement. What's remarkable about this stage is that it breaks the link between the Ledger and physical currency. In principle, if everyone in the world used this Ledger, you could spend your entire life sending and receiving money on it without ever having to convert it to US dollars. To underline this point, let's start referring to ledger amounts as "LedgerDollars," or LD for short. Of course, you are free to swap LedgerDollars for actual US dollars; for example, Alice may send Bob a $10 note in return for his entering and signing the transaction "Bob pays Alice 10 LedgerDollars" to the common ledger. However, such exchanges are not guaranteed by the protocol. It's now more like exchanging dollars for euros or any other money on the open market; it's just its own thing. The first thing to grasp about Bitcoin, or any other cryptocurrency, is this: What exactly is it? It's a ledger, after all, and the currency is the history of transactions. Of course, with Bitcoin, money does not enter the Ledger when individuals purchase it with cash. There is an even greater distinction between our existing system of LedgerDollars and how cryptocurrencies operate. So far, I've stated that this ledger is a public space, similar to a website, where anybody may contribute new lines.

However, this necessitates putting your faith in a central spot. Who, specifically, hosts the website? Who decides the regulations for adding more lines? We'll make everyone retain their own copy of the ledger to remove that piece of trust. Then you broadcast a transaction, such as "Alice pays Bob 100 LedgerDollars," into the globe for everyone to hear and record on their own private Ledgers. However, unless we do anything else, this system will be insanely horrible. How do you get everyone to agree on which ledger is correct? How can Bob be certain that everyone else got and believes the transaction "Alice pays Bob 10 LedgerDollars" when he receives it? That he'll be able to utilize those ten LedgerDollars to make a deal with Charlie later on. Consider yourself simply listening to transactions being aired. How do you know everyone else is logging the same transactions in the same order? We've now discovered an intriguing puzzle: Can you devise a mechanism for accepting or rejecting transactions and in what sequence, such that you can be certain that anybody else following the same process has a personal ledger that looks exactly like yours? This was addressed in the initial Bitcoin whitepaper. At a high level, Bitcoin provides the answer of trusting whatever ledger has the greatest computational power put into it. This is accomplished through the use of a "cryptographic hash function."

The main notion is that if you utilize computational labor as a criterion for what to trust, you may make fraudulent transactions and conflicting ledgers cost an infeasible amount of compute. This is going far beyond what someone would need to know merely to utilize a currency like this. But it's a pretty intriguing notion, and understanding it means understanding the essence of Bitcoin and other cryptocurrencies. A hash function accepts any type of message or file and returns a string of bits with a specified length, such as 256 bits.

This output is known as the message's "hash" or "digest," and it is intended to appear random. It isn't random; it always produces the same result for a given input. However, the concept is that if you modify the input slightly, like by changing only one of the letters, the resultant hash changes altogether. In reality, with the hash function SHA256, the way the result changes when the input is changed slightly is completely unexpected. It's not just any hash function; this is a cryptographic hash function. That is, it is impossible to compute in the other way. If I show you a precise string of 1's and 0's and ask you to discover an input message whose SHA256 hash yields this same string of bits, you will have no choice but to guess and check.

You could assume you might reverse engineer the required input by delving into the specifics of how the function works, but no one has ever succeeded. Surprisingly, there is no proof that it is difficult to compute in the other way, despite the fact that cryptographic hash functions are used in a large portion of current security. If you look at the algorithms that underpin the secure connection that your browser is establishing with a bank, for example, you will most likely find a name like SHA256. For the time being, our attention will be only on how such a function may demonstrate that a certain set of transactions is connected with a significant amount of computing work. Assume someone offers you a list of transactions and says, "I discovered a peculiar number such that when you put this number at the end of the list of transactions and apply SHA256 to the entire thing, the first 30 bits of the result are zeros." How difficult do you believe it was for them to find that number? For a random message, the likelihood that the hash begins with 30 consecutive zeros is 1 in 230, or nearly 1 in a billion. Because SHA256 is a cryptographic hash algorithm, the only method to find a unique number like this is to guess and double-check. So this individual very definitely had to sift through a billion different numbers before coming to this one.

Once you have the number, you can immediately confirm that this hash does indeed begin with 30 zeros. In other words, you can verify they put in a lot of effort without having to put in the same amount of effort yourself. This is known as "proof of labor." Notably, all of this effort is inextricably linked to that list of transactions. If you changed even one of the transactions, the hash would be entirely changed, and you'd have to go through another billion guesses to discover a new proof of work, a new number that makes the hash of the amended list plus this new number starts with 30 zeros. Now consider our distributed ledger situation. Everyone is broadcasting transactions, and we need a means for everyone to agree on the right ledger.

The original Bitcoin paper's central principle is for everyone to believe whatever ledger has the greatest labor put into it. This works by first organizing a given ledger into blocks, with each block including a list of transactions and a proof of work. That is a unique integer such that the hash of the entire block begins with a string of zeros. For the time being, let's suppose it has to begin with 60 zeros, but I'll return to how you may determine that amount later. A block is only regarded legitimate if it has proof of work, just as a transaction is only considered genuine if it is signed by the sender. Similarly, to ensure that these blocks are ordered consistently, we'll require that each block contain the hash of the preceding block. If you edit any block or try to swap the order of two blocks, it will change the block following it, which will change the hash of that block, which will affect the next block, and so on. That would need repeating all of the work, in order to obtain a new special number for each of these blocks, causing their hashes to begin with 60 zeros. Because the blocks are linked together in this manner, it is frequently referred to as a "Blockchain" rather than a "Ledger." We will now allow anyone in the globe to be a "block maker" as part of our new protocol. This implies they'll listen for broadcast transactions, aggregate them into a block, then conduct a bunch of effort to locate the particular number that causes the hash of this block to begin with 60 zeros, then broadcast the block they found. To reward a block maker for all of her efforts, we'll let her to place a unique transaction at the top of the block in which she earns, says, 10 LedgerDollars out of thin air. This is known as the block reward. It's an exemption to our typical rules regarding whether or not to accept transactions; because it doesn't originate from anybody, it doesn't need to be signed. It also implies that with each new block, the overall quantity of LedgerDollars in our economy grows. Because it demands a lot of labor and puts fresh cash into the system, creating blocks is commonly referred to as "mining."

When you hear or read about miners, bear in mind that what they're really doing is building blocks, broadcasting those blocks, and being rewarded with additional money for it. Each block, from the perspective of the miners, is like a little lottery, with everyone guessing numbers as rapidly as they can until one lucky individual finds one that causes the hash of the block to begin with many zeros, and is paid for doing so. Instead of listening for transactions, users of this system will instead listen for new blocks broadcast by miners, which will update their own copy of the blockchain. The key difference is that if you hear of two distinct blockchains with conflicting transaction histories, you choose the one with the longest history and the most work put into it. Wait till you hear of an extra block that makes one longer if there is a tie. So, even if there is no central authority and everyone keeps their own copy of the blockchain, if everyone agrees to give priority to the blockchain with the greatest work put into it, we have a mechanism to achieve decentralized consensus.

It's useful to walk through what it would take to trick someone into this system to show why this provides for a trustworthy system and when you should believe that payment is authentic. If Alice wishes to deceive Bob, she may send him a false block that involves her giving him 100 LedgerDollars but does not broadcast the block to the rest of the network. Everyone else will assume she still has those 100 LedgerDollars. To do so, she'd have to discover a legitimate proof of work before all the other miners, each of whom was working on their own block. That is something that may happen! Perhaps Alice will be the first to win this small lotto. However, Bob will continue to receive broadcasts from other miners, so in order to keep him believing the fake block, Alice would have to undertake all of the work herself to maintain adding blocks to this particular fork in Bob's blockchain that differs from what the rest of the miners are hearing. Remember, according to protocol, Bob always trusts the longest chain he is aware of. Alice might be able to keep this going for a few blocks if she manages to locate blocks faster than the rest of the miners on the network combined.

However, until Alice possesses close to 50% of all miners' processing capacity, the possibility that the blockchain that all other miners are working on develops faster than the single false blockchain that Alice is feeding Bob becomes overwhelming. As a result, Bob will eventually reject what Alice is saying in favor of the larger chain that everyone else is working on. That implies you shouldn't always believe a new block that you hear right away. You should instead wait for several new blocks to be added on top of it. If you haven't heard of any other blockchains, you may be certain that this block is part of the same chain that everyone else is using. With that, we've covered all of the major points. This distributed ledger system based on proof of work is how the Bitcoin protocol and many other cryptocurrencies operate. There are only a few details to work out. I said before that the proof of work may be to identify a specific integer such that the hash of the block begins with 60 zeros. The Bitcoin protocol operates by changing the number of zeros on a regular basis, such that it should take about 10 minutes to discover a block on average. As more miners join the network, the task becomes increasingly difficult, to the point that this little lottery only has one winner every 10 minutes. Many of the newer coins have significantly lower block times. All of the money in Bitcoin is derived from some form of the block reward. This pays out 50 Bitcoin for each block.

There's a great site called "block explorer" where you can look through the Bitcoin blockchain, and the first few blocks on the chain contain no transactions other than the miner's 50 Bitcoin reward. That reward is cut in half every 210,000 blocks or roughly every 4 years. Because this reward diminishes geometrically over time, there will never be more than 21 million Bitcoin. However, this does not mean that miners will no longer be able to earn a living. Miners can earn transaction fees in addition to the block reward. The way this works is that anytime you make a payment, you may optionally include a tiny transaction fee with it, which will be distributed to the miner of the block that includes that payment. This might be done to motivate miners to include the transaction you publish in the following block.

Each Bitcoin block is limited to approximately 2,400 transactions, which many critics argue is overly restrictive. In comparison, Visa handles around 1,700 transactions per second on average, with a capacity of more than 24,000 transactions per second. Slower Bitcoin processing equals higher transaction fees because it impacts which transactions miners choose to include in subsequent blocks. This is far from an exhaustive examination of cryptocurrencies. There are numerous complexities and different design options that I haven't addressed, but hopefully, this provides a sturdy trunk of understanding for anyone seeking to add a few more branches with more reading. A lot of money has begun to flow towards cryptocurrencies, and although I don't want to make any assertions about whether this is a good or terrible investment, I do believe it would be beneficial for individuals going into this game to understand the principles of the technology.

CHAPTER 8:

HOW TO INVEST IN BITCOIN SAFELY

In this chapter, I'll go over how to start investing in Bitcoin step by step, how to keep it safe and secure, how to create passive income and interest with it, and most importantly, how to pay your taxes with it automatically, which is really valuable to know. The cryptocurrency field isn't renowned for being the most ethical of places, so I want to make sure that no one is taken advantage of. After all, half of the world thinks Bitcoin is a hoax no matter what you tell them, and the other half thinks it's a religion, so don't insult them. I'm somewhere in the center since I believe that putting all of your money in it is a horrible idea, but investing none of your money is equally awful. Bitcoin has been around for over ten years and has withstood every technological test that we have thrown at it, but at the end of the day, we don't know what's around the corner, and while Bitcoin is likely to be the most valuable and the one with the most potential, technology is bound to be disrupted in the future, and I do believe that Bitcoin is here to stay for a long time but invest only what you're comfortable with. Step one is to find the best brokerage. The answer is determined by what you value the most.

For me, it means safety and security, ease of use, and value, so I want to ensure that the money I spend is, first and foremost, absolutely secure. Second, I want to make sure that the interface does not appear overly difficult. Three, I want to be sure I'm receiving a decent deal and not overpaying in fees. I'm willing to spend a little more on an extra layer of security. All of these brokerages, regardless of who you choose, require two things: AML and KYC. Know Your Customer and Anti-Money Laundering regulations must be observed. That means you'll need your ID, your address, your phone number, and everything else necessary for conventional brokerage. Gemini and Coinbase are two of my favorite brokerages. I have accounts with each of them, and they are both fantastic. You can't go wrong with either one, and the sign-up process is nearly the same, but in general, the less information you offer to them, the lower your limit to purchase and sell Bitcoin will be. The more information you submit, the greater your restriction. I'll describe the sign-up procedure in Gemini because that's the brokerage I use the most. The first thing it will ask you for is your first name, last name, email address, password, and phone number, followed by a phone number. The following page will request a passport photo or a driver's license ID, followed by a passport number and a physical postal address. Once you've finished that, you're ready to leave. After you've joined up, the next step is to ensure that our account is safe and secure and that no one can steal our Bitcoins, which you can accomplish by heading to the app store and installing the free program "authy." This is only to ensure that even if someone gets our login or email and passwords, they won't be able to log in and do anything bad unless they have physical access to our phone, which we hope they don't. After you've downloaded "authy," Gemini should appear in the app

on its own. You may click on it to view a seven-digit number that will continually renew itself every 20 seconds. Gemini will then ask for the seven-digit number on a regular basis to ensure it's you, but once you're satisfied, we'll go on to the next level. First, you must fund your account, and Coinbase offers a variety of ways to do so, including credit cards. However, never buy Bitcoin using a credit or debit card since the fees are exorbitantly high at 3.49 percent. That is high since, for comparison, the stock market earns 7% per year, and you will only spend half of that upfront to begin investing. Never, ever pay 3.49 percent for anything. Instead, link your bank account. There are two ways to do this: the manual way, in which they send you pennies and you confirm ownership of your bank account with them, and the automatic way, in which you go to the upper right hand corner, click on "account settings," then "funding sources," and then click on the "automatically link bank account" option. This is accomplished through the use of third-party software integration, which automatically links everything, and these brokerages do not have access to your bank accounts. It can only be done through "plaid," an extremely safe and secure service. I have two accounts linked, but doing it manually will take a few days versus utilizing "plaid," which is virtually instant. This is how you may move money from your bank into the brokerage after you've connected your financing sources. Transfer the funds to Gemini by clicking on the transfer button. You'll be asked to choose a currency at this time. You can just use US dollars, and in the deposit method, you'll find two options: bank transfer, which restricts you to $15,000 a day and would cover most people, but if you're doing more than that, you'll have to use the wire transfer option. When you press the proceed button, you'll see a variety of instructions, but one thing you should really pay attention to is the reference code. That informs Gemini which accounts to put your money into so that it doesn't land up in the hands of a random individual.

That is your one-of-a-kind identification. If you're from Europe, you won't be using wire transfers. You'll be utilizing something called the Sepa transfer, and if you're Canadian, you'll be using PayPal to withdraw your money and then using Debit cards to buy it, which isn't the best choice but it'll suffice. Let's finally buy some Bitcoin now that you've filled your account. On the home page, you may invest in a variety of currencies, but the ones you should be most concerned with are Bitcoin and Ethereum. They are the most respectable enterprises in our field; they were the first, and they have the highest future development potential. If you want to buy Bitcoin on this page, all you have to do is click on it and then select whether you want to buy it once, daily, weekly, or whatever you want and enter how much depending on how much you want to invest and then click on "review order" and at this point, you can enter in the payment method and choose which one you want and then place the order. That's all. Before we move on, there's something really crucial I want you to realize because if you believe you're going to become a billionaire with Bitcoin overnight and then cash out, there are a few limits you may encounter, and here they are. There is a $15,000 daily limit but a $30,000 monthly maximum if you use Gemini's transfer mechanism, and a $100,000 daily limit if you withdraw money to your bank account. If you want to buy Bitcoin with a debit card, you can only buy $500 at a time.

That's crucial to know if you're extremely thrilled to purchase Bitcoin only to discover that you can't buy a full one with your debit card or whatever else you're going to use. If you use Coinbase, the structure is similar in that it relies on the amount of verification. The more information you provide to those sites, such as your passport and social security number, the greater your limit will be. Now that you've hopefully purchased a Bitcoin, let's move on to the next stage since once the Bitcoin is in your account, you have two options. Either the cold path or my personal favorite, the hot route, in which you may keep your Bitcoin on the exchange itself, which is dubbed a hot wallet.

The advantage of doing this is that you have quick liquidity because your Bitcoin can be sold straight away, exchanged for a new currency, and earned interest on a separate website, all of which are fantastic. The disadvantage is that you must trust that such exchanges or businesses will keep your money safe from computer hackers who try to steal it. The second option is to use cold storage, which involves taking our currencies offline and transferring them to the blockchain via a device called the Ledger Nano wallet. But first, I'd want to show you the hot wallet approach, which is what I use since I believe your money should always be collecting interest and providing you passive income, thus blockfy.com is what I prefer to utilize. If you decide to pursue this way, please take the time to thoroughly follow the next few instructions. Go to the top of the page and look for "deposit." Click on it and then choose the coin you purchased from the brokerage. I'm using Bitcoin as an example, so that's what I'd use, and there's a link at the bottom. That is the address of your public wallet. You may copy the number by clicking a little page icon and pasting it into your brokerage. Back to Gemini, if you try to transfer then withdraw from Gemini, you may pick the currency, and then when it asks for the destination, you paste the code you received from Blockfy. Then you want to choose the amount you want to transfer and make sure that your wallet address from Gemini matches what it appears in blockfy because if anything is amiss, even a single digit, your money will just go under the table, which you don't want since it will never return. It will be the most anxious few minutes of your life once you transfer the money. Please exercise extreme caution. You won't know whether you accomplished it correctly for the next few minutes, so send over a little portion first to ensure that you didn't send the complete balance over and lose it, and then send over the remainder of the money. The concept of collecting interest on cryptocurrency is not unique to blockfy.

There's also Celsius.network and Nexo.io, but the reason I like blockfy so much is that they connect so well with Gemini, and the majority of the money stored on blockfy is really stored in a cold storage wallet with Gemini. The two have collaborated on this, and another reason I have faith in Blockfy is that if you go to their investor relations website, you can see all of the money that is behind them. This venture capital money is extremely substantial and very known in the sector, and I feel that they are making the right judgments, so if blockfy disappears, it would not only make them seem bad but also the investors themselves, which is why I've picked blockfy. But don't only utilize the same firms I use; I just want to provide you with as many diverse alternatives as possible. If you're thinking to yourself, "This is still way too confusing," and you just want to keep your Bitcoin on the exchange, I'll tell you that you're still assuming excessive risk without reaping any of the benefits of interest. If you're going to do that, put your funds to a cold storage offline wallet instead. This essentially guarantees that your money will be kept in the safest location imaginable, which is literally on the blockchain, which no one has been able to break into so far. So, let me tell you a bit more about hardware wallets.

It's a $57 gadget that you can acquire directly from Ledger at https://shop.ledger.com/products/ledger-nano-s, but you should get one as soon as your crypto balance hits $1,000. There are a number of tutorials on the Ledger website for getting this gadget up and running, and after you obtain it, you'll get a list of key phrases and words that it will ask you to write down and hide somewhere. Never snap a photo of these terms, never post them, and never have someone else do it for you. Not a fiduciary, not a tax expert, and not a banker, because if someone knows your key phrase list, they may access your wallet at any moment and take your money. As soon as you write that down, hide it somewhere and forget about it, since even if you lose or destroy the hardware wallet, you'll still be able to access your Bitcoin as long as you have your tiny hidden list. Another reason I don't advocate using Robinhood to acquire crypto is that you can't withdraw your coins and put them into anything like this. Now that you're a crypto expert and know all there is to know about Bitcoin, if you've ever bought, sold, or traded it, you'll most likely have to pay taxes on it, and here is how you can do it effortlessly. I use app.taxbit.com and a few others, but this one is very wonderful since it automatically interacts with practically every account that I use, and you enable access for these websites to observe your crypto accounts, but they can't make any changes.

They are unable to buy, sell, or steal them for themselves. It's only an auditing position. In Gemini's case, you can just give them an auditor role and they'll be able to go in there automatically and calculate all of your buys, all of your sells, and it just aggregates everything for you, and then you can print out that sheet, give it to your tax person, and everything is automatically calculated. It's not something I've ever done before, but for the interest of completeness, you should be aware of the following information. If you value privacy and the right to purchase, trade, and exchange bitcoin without the knowledge or cooperation of the government, there are two websites that enable you to do so. They are localcryptos.com and local.bitcoin.com, and you can think of them as the craigslist or offer up of the crypto World in that your local people can just meet up exchange money, you can get the crypto right away, and you get tax shelter, but in exchange, you'll be paying a much higher premium and you're definitely taking a risk. At the end of the day, I don't condone doing this, but when it comes to a relationship with the IRS, everyone to their own. Simply utilize your abilities for good, be responsible, be safe, and pay your taxes.

CHAPTER 9:

THE FUTURE OF BITCOIN MINING

There's a reason Bitcoin is frequently referred to as digital gold. This is due to the fact that, like gold, Bitcoin has a limited quantity, and whereas gold has been used in electronics and medicine, Bitcoin has applications as a network that allows you to safely transmit and hold value without the use of an intermediary. The mix of scarcity and usefulness is what gives gold and Bitcoin such high value. But there is one significant distinction between gold and Bitcoin:

Bitcoin relies on the generation of new Bitcoin to compensate miners who process transactions on the network. When all of the gold is produced, it may still be exchanged, but what happens when all of the Bitcoin is mined? Will the Bitcoin network fall, bringing the whole cryptocurrency industry down with it? How much time do we have until this occurs? Is there a way to solve this problem? Don't worry, I'll address all of these things and more in this chapter. You may be well-versed on Bitcoin, but I want to make sure we're all on the same page. As a result, I'm going to start with a fast review of some of the key themes. On January 3, 2009, the first Bitcoin block was mined, purportedly by Bitcoin's creator, Satoshi Nakamoto. The genesis block of Bitcoin had a secret message that read The Times 3rd of January 2009; "Chancellor on the verge of the second bailout for banks," which was the headline of the London Times on that day. In addition to this message, the first block of Bitcoin featured the first cryptocurrency mining reward of 50 BTC. The reason for having BTC coins at all is to provide an economic incentive for miners to maintain the network. BTC is awarded as a reward for completing transactions that are recorded in blocks on the Bitcoin network. Every time a new Bitcoin block is mined, new BTC are created.

The Bitcoin programming guarantees that this occurs about every 10 minutes by altering the mining difficulty based on the number of miners. Bitcoin's block reward was 50 BTC until November 28, 2012, when it was halved, decreasing the block reward from 50 BTC to 25 BTC. Every 210,000 blocks, Bitcoin is halved.

Although this officially equals four years, the real amount is slightly different. The Bitcoin halvings are notable because the rapid drop in new BTC supply they create is anticipated to eventually induce a surge in BTC price, providing BTC demand remains constant or grows after the halving. For example, the most recent Bitcoin halving occurred in May of 2020, and it's evident that we're presently in a bull market. These Bitcoin halvings aren't going to last forever.

This is due to the fact that the maximum quantity of BTC that may ever be mined is 21 million, and this restriction is encoded into the Bitcoin code. Satoshi Nakamoto most likely chose this restriction for mathematical reasons. It's also likely that he determined this limit based on the M1 money supply in the world, which was roughly 21 trillion dollars in 2009. If this is the case, Satoshi planned for each BTC to someday be worth a million dollars. When will the final Bitcoin be mined? If you've ever Googled this query, you've probably gotten the same answer as everyone else, which is the year 2140.

You would be accurate if you believe that looks like a long period considering the current circulating quantity of BTC, which is roughly 18.6 million. When you dive deeper into the math employed by most writers to get at this amount, you'll see that it implies Bitcoin halve every four years, which is not exactly right. They aren't quite four years apart in age. They are, in reality, just approximately three years and nine months apart. Fortunately, someone else completed the math and discovered that if this three-year and nine month gap persists, the final BTC would most likely be mined towards the end of 2078. Nobody has claimed that when there are no more BTC to mine, there would be no longer economic incentives for miners, and the Bitcoin network will die, and because the whole cryptocurrency market is based on Bitcoin, every cryptocurrency will fall to zero.

To begin with, Bitcoin's dominance has been steadily declining since 2017, implying that BTC will not be the leading cryptocurrency by market size in 2078. That is, the remainder of the cryptocurrency market will no longer be as reliant on it. Furthermore, in addition to the rewards from each new Bitcoin block, BTC miners receive fees for processing transactions. If you open a Bitcoin block explorer, you can check how much BTC a miner got from the block they mined by deducting the current BTC rewards from the total block reward. In this scenario, we can observe that miners make anything from 0.5 to 1 BTC each block just from transaction fees. Many individuals think that when the BTC mining rewards run out, the transaction fees will be sufficient to keep the Bitcoin network running. There's only one problem with this theory. Given that Bitcoin can only execute about seven transactions per second, it's doubtful that it will become the payment network of choice for small-scale transactions such as buying a pack of gum at the grocery store.

The transaction costs alone would be several times the amount you were spending. Bitcoin developers are very aware of the rising cost of transaction fees and their impact on micropayments. It's why, for years, they've been working on layer 2 scaling solutions like the lightning network. Layer 2 alternatives, such as the lightning network, have the disadvantage of reducing the number of transactions that occur on the Bitcoin blockchain. They instead only send transactions to the Bitcoin blockchain when a payment channel is formed and terminated. Because there are fewer transactions, the fees for creating and closing these payment channels must be extremely high in order for Bitcoin miners to be lucrative and operating. After all, they must cover the costs of the hardware and power necessary to keep the Bitcoin network running. These high fees would then put pressure on layer twos, such as the lightning network, to minimize the opening and closing of their payment channels, resulting in a vicious cycle that would either bankrupt Bitcoin miners or corrupt the Bitcoin network due to an over-reliance on less secure layer 2 solutions. Bitcoin maximalists would disagree, but it becomes apparent that Bitcoin's main stick is as a store of wealth, rather than as a currency network utilized for day-to-day transactions. As a result, contrary to what Satoshi Nakamoto envisioned, it is far more probable that BTC will be seldom transferred about in the future. This implies that if Bitcoin is to live beyond the data that no longer rewards miners with BTC, it must be able to do so without depending on transaction fees. Here are a few potential answers. Sustaining a proof-of-work cryptocurrency network like Bitcoin necessitates a significant amount of processing power and electricity. These constitute the majority of the operational expenditures of cryptocurrency miners worldwide, and it is for this reason that many mining farms move to nations and areas with inexpensive energy, especially China and portions of North America.

Despite the fact that the Bitcoin network is unlikely to survive only on transaction fees, this is predicated on the premise that the cost of cryptocurrency mining will remain the same after we run out of BTC. However, in the following decades, it is extremely possible that energy will grow cheaper and technology will become more efficient. Although green energy solutions are still in their infancy, green energy companies in the UK are actively mining cryptocurrency with their extra electricity. This increases the profitability of their services and helps them to grow their green energy activities. Much to the embarrassment of those who say that bitcoin mining is destroying the earth. Furthermore, Bitcoin mining machines are becoming more economical and efficient with each passing year. Cheap energy and efficient gear would make it simple for Bitcoin miners to be profitable solely on transaction fees, further decentralizing Bitcoin as more miners joined the network to partake in those fees. Economic incentives aren't the only thing that may save the Bitcoin network.

Many have speculated about when the public sector would follow corporations like Microstrategy in acquiring Bitcoin as part of their treasury reserves. Given that the mayor of Miami has explored investing 1% of the city's treasury reserves in BTC, it appears that it's just a matter of time. If and when towns, states, and even countries start holding Bitcoin as part of their reserves, they will have every motivation in the world to keep the Bitcoin network safe and operating. If public institutions retain BTC after the final one is mined and discover that Bitcoin miners are starting to shut down their mining rigs due to a lack of revenues, they will not hesitate to support those miners or even launch their own mining operations in order to keep the Bitcoin network running. Similarly, if a sufficient number of individuals in a given nation own BTC and the Bitcoin network is under threat, they might put pressure on their government to provide subsidies for Bitcoin mining farms in order to defend their money.

These protectionist measures may not originate only from the public sector. If a sufficient number of private corporations begin to hold big quantities of BTC, they, too, will have the motivation to rush in and ensure that the Bitcoin network remains working. This notion of having skin in the game pushes users to build Bitcoin nodes, which keep copies of transaction histories on the Bitcoin blockchain to promote the network's decentralization. Even though they do not get transaction fees or mining incentives for the vital service they serve, there are over 6,400 Bitcoin nodes. Another possibility is that the whole Bitcoin network may just transfer to a smart contract blockchain like Ethereum. Currently, about 7% of Bitcoin's circulating supply resides on Ethereum as an ERC20 token known as WBTC and RenBTC. This is due to a process known as "wrapping," which locks a coin on its original blockchain in order to generate an equivalent number of ERC20 tokens on Ethereum. Wrapped BTC has grown in popularity over the last year for two reasons. First, you may use wrapped BTC in multiple DeFi protocols to earn interest on your BTC. Second, moving WBTC is frequently faster and less expensive than moving genuine BTC. It's also not simply Ethereum. Cardano and Polkadot are both slated to provide smart contract functionality this year, with Polkadot announcing in October 2020 that they will enable wrapped BTC on their network in Q1 of this year as Polka BTC. Ethereum, Polkadot, and Cardano would be wildly decentralized by the time the BTC awards ran out. In other words, network security would be minimal to non-existent.

The only difficulty would be moving all of the BTC on the Bitcoin blockchain to Ethereum, which is unlikely to be something that every BTC holder would be ready to undertake. However, it is extremely possible because BTC may be burnt on the Bitcoin blockchain by transferring it to a phony address. These are the kind of addresses that you may have unintentionally sent funds to when you were a crypto novice. An Ethereum smart contract might monitor transactions sent to these phony Bitcoin addresses and generate an equivalent amount of BTC in the form of ERC20 tokens.

There is, of course, one more option, which is to expand the supply of BTC. I know what you're thinking: I assumed 21 million was a protocol-defined maximum, and you're correct. It is, however, technically feasible to raise this limit. So long as there is agreement from the quote economic majority, which is more than simply 51 percent of miners. This comprises all economic actors, including miners, developers, users, merchants, and so on. The vast majority of these organizations must agree on any important modification to the Bitcoin network for it to pass, even though the changes to Bitcoin's code are ultimately implemented by engineers at firms like Blockstream. Consider the following if you're wondering why. When some members of the Bitcoin community proposed increasing the size of Bitcoin's blocks in order to handle more transactions, not everyone agreed. As a result, the Bitcoin network forked in the summer of 2017. The new Bitcoin blockchain, with its higher block size, was dubbed Bitcoin cash. Bitcoin Cash forked again in November 2018 to become Bitcoin Satoshi Vision, often known as Bitcoin SV. Even if the current economic players in Bitcoin's ecosystem would never designate a Bitcoin blockchain with a bigger BTC supply as the actual Bitcoin, this might alter in the next years and decades. It is absolutely feasible that the maximum supply of BTC will be raised at some point in the future.

Bitcoin, it turns out, has more than one means of surviving long after the BTC mining incentives have run out. It's crazy that this will most likely happen in my lifetime, but the improvements we'll see in the cryptocurrency field between now and then will be even weirder. After all, the cryptocurrency field isn't the only location where innovation is taking place. Many of these new discoveries will be relevant to the Bitcoin network and have the potential to build an altogether new business model for cryptocurrency mining.

This is going to be important since I don't see how the Bitcoin network can support itself just on transaction fees, and layer 2 solutions will not assist at all. There is no shortage of competition in the cryptocurrency market when it comes to payments, and many of these rival projects perform far better than Bitcoin. Bitcoin is a store of value, and both public and private organizations are beginning to recognize this. It would not surprise me in the least if a large city state or government listed BTC as one of its reserve assets by the end of the year. Even if that information is released, it will serve as a conclusive assurance that the Bitcoin network is here to stay. Surprisingly, it appears that BTC currencies are slowly but steadily relocating to better pastures. By the end of the decade, it is extremely likely that the bulk of all current BTC will be locked on smart contract blockchains like Ethereum, Polkadot, and Cardano. At the end of the day, everything is about economic incentives, and it is natural for consumers to want to transfer their store of value assets to platforms where they may earn interest.

For the time being, raising the maximum supply of BTC is just out of the question. Bitcoin is the world's most secure network. It has millions of users, millions of miners, and tens of thousands of the world's greatest brains working on it 24 hours a day, seven days a week. This is a truth that no amount of enjoyment can change.

CHAPTER 10:

HOW TO TRADE USING FTX, HUOBI & BNB TOKENS

If you've been paying attention to the cryptocurrency leader boards, you've undoubtedly noticed an odd pattern. Exchange tokens are rapidly ascending the ranks, with virtually all of them experiencing exponential growth in recent months. This is hardly unexpected considering that these tokens provide benefits to dealers on their individual exchanges and that trading volumes on centralized exchanges have surged in tandem with the bull market. However, these trade tokens are utilized for more than just that.

Many cryptocurrency exchanges are also developing their own centralized DeFi ecosystems, which introduce a completely new layer of use cases for exchange tokens, particularly as payment for network fees. If the performance of Binance's BNB is any indicator, these exchange tokens maybe just getting started. So, in this chapter, I'll take a closer look at the Binance coin, as well as the Huobi token and the FTX token, to see whether they have any real promise or if all of the current price activity is just a ruse. Binance is the world's largest cryptocurrency exchange by trading volume. It was formed in China and relocated out of the country in 2017, prior to the Chinese government's ban on cryptocurrency trading. Binance is headquartered in Malta, however, it is formally registered in the Cayman Islands and the Seychelles. BNB is a cryptocurrency that is utilized in the Binance ecosystem. BNB provides a plethora of use cases given the breadth of this ecosystem. To begin with, more than 90% of Binance staff are paid in BNB. On the Binance exchange, traders can receive a 25% reduction on trading costs when paying in BNB; however, according to the BNB white paper, this trading discount will reduce over time, and BNB will no longer give any incentives to traders after July 2022. On the Binance exchange, there are over 100 trading pairs using BNB that have a lot of volume. BNB may also be used to make ordinary purchases using the Binance Card, and it will be one of the five cryptocurrencies supported by the future Binance pay service.

Binance Pay is billed as a "crypto-based PayPal competitor" and is set to launch in alpha early next year. Having said that, BNB is already being used to book flights and hotels, purchase music and gift cards, and even pay for website servers. Merchants can accept BNB as payment using a variety of plugins, including "Coin payments" and "Now payments." However, it appears that the majority of BNB demand is coming from its use in Binance's thriving cDeFi ecosystem, where it's utilized for trading collateral for lending liquidity mining, and, of course, gas fees. BNB debuted as an ERC20 coin and was sold during Binance's ICO round in the summer of 2017. This resulted in the sale of 100 million BNB at a cost of roughly 11 cents per unit, raising approximately 15 million dollars in total. The Binance team received 80 million BNB, while angel investors received another 20 million BNB. BNB has an initial supply of 200 million and is deflationary owing to Binance's quarterly burns.

Binance utilizes 20% of its quarterly income to burn BNB in this case. This process will be repeated until the supply of BNB exceeds 100 million. So far, little less than 30 million BNB have been destroyed, with the most recent fire being in January 2022. Binance CEO CZ said that he wishes to expedite the burning of BNB in order to meet the 100 million objective within the next five to eight years. It is worth noting that it is unclear where these burnt tokens are coming from. In April 2019, references to Binance's "repurchasing intentions" were deleted from the Binance white paper. To add to the uncertainty, Binance said the same month that the 80 million BNB team allotment will be burned as part of their ongoing quarterly burns, rather than investing it over four years. Binance appears to be holding little more than 53 million BNB in four wallets on the Binance chain, which is now the native chain of the BNB currency.

This 27 million BNB differential corresponds quite well to the quantity of BNB consumed thus far. In addition to the Binance chain, BNB exists as a BEP20 token on the Binance smart chain, where it is used to pay for gas costs when interacting with different cDeFi protocols. The entire value locked in these cDeFi protocols matches rather well to the price action of BNB, which has increased by a comfortable 5x since the beginning of 2022. BNB is the most valuable of all exchange tokens and by a wide margin. While it may continue to expand, this growth appears to be dependent on Binance's cDeFi ecosystem, and acceptance of those protocols appears to be based on the low gas fees supplied by the Binance smart chain. Binance's cDeFi ecosystem's only selling point is its low gas fees. There does not appear to be much creativity or innovation in that field.

The majority of the protocols are simply copied copies of popular Ethereum DeFi protocols, which is where most of the DeFi innovation is still taking place, despite the high gas prices. However, Ethereum is reportedly just weeks away from passing EIP1559, which would effectively fix all of the concerns with gas costs and send the price of Eth skyrocketing. When EIP1559 is implemented, DeFi Degen will have little reason to remain on the Binance smart chain. But, until that day arrives, BNB will continue to expand. Moving on, Huobi is the second largest cryptocurrency exchange in terms of trade volume. It was established in 2013 in China and is registered in Seychelles.

In contrast to Binance, Huobi chose to restructure its business model in reaction to the Chinese government's 2017 ban. Huobi China is currently a consultancy firm specializing in blockchain technology. Huobi Group controls a number of cryptocurrency exchanges across the world, including Huobi Global, Huobi Career, and the soon-to-be-restored Huobi US. Huobi is also a publicly listed firm on the Hong Kong Stock Exchange, and Huobi CEO Leon Lee appears to have excellent relations with the Chinese government.

The Huobi token is a cryptocurrency that is utilized within the Huobi ecosystem. Holding the Huobi token in your exchange wallet might provide you with a trading fee savings of up to 65 percent on Huobi cryptocurrency exchanges. It also grants you access to unique token sales and allows you to win incentives on cryptocurrency-related special events such as Bitcoin pizza day. The Huobi token, like BNB, may be used to pay for services from a variety of businesses, however, the list is not as wide. In contrast to BNB, holding the Huobi token entitles you to vote on any proposed modifications to the cryptocurrency exchange. While Huobi has been working with the Nervous network on a smart contract blockchain named the Huobi chain since 2019, the Huobi chain has yet to escape its test net phase. In contrast to Binance's cDeFi and DeFi in general, the Huobi chain is intended to be Chinese regulatory compliance and will require KYC to use. According to a Decrypt article, the major characteristic of the Huobi chain is reported that it allows the Chinese government to establish a regulator node that gives the government unrestricted access to all on-chain data.

To suggest that many people will be uncomfortable with it is an understatement. Still, Chinese investors are clamoring for DeFi, and providing them with a legal means to be DeFi Degen is unquestionably valuable. However, it is unclear if the Huobi token will play a role in Huobi's DeFi ecosystem. This is because the Huobi token is an ERC20 token that was sold in a method that regulators are unlikely to approve of. In February 2018, Huobi adopted a rewards card system instead of an ICO. Users of the exchange may buy rewards cards that would entitle them to "free Huobi tokens." The numbers are a little convoluted, but the average price of these rewards card purchases was roughly $1.50 per Huobi token. Huobi gave out 300 million Huobi tokens for free, and Huobi reportedly made $300 million dollars through point card sales. The maximum quantity of the Huobi token is 500 million. The remaining 200 million Huobi tokens were divided as follows: 100 million were set aside for future rewards, and 100 million were assigned to the Huobi team with a four-year vesting schedule. Huobi, like Binance and BNB, devotes 20% of its income to the burning of Huobi tokens. Unlike Binance, Huobi says that 15% of this money is utilized to acquire and burn circulating supply tokens, while the remaining 5% is used to burn Huobi tokens allotted to the team. As a result, Huobi's token burning are anticipated to have a higher influence on the price than Binance's BNB burns. Huobi acquired and burnt Huobi tokens quarterly until 2020 when they shifted to monthly burning. Huobi has burnt 250 million Huobi tokens so far, and this burning is expected to continue until all Huobi tokens are consumed.

The Huobi token is the second most valuable exchange token in terms of market capitalization. In terms of price action, it has done almost as well as BNB since the beginning of the year. This is odd given that the Huobi coin does not have nearly as much market demand as BNB. This price movement may be attributed almost exclusively to Huobi's purchase and burning of Huobi tokens. This conduct virtually assures that the Huobi token's price will rise. But I'm curious how long this gravy train will stay on the tracks. Despite the CEO's close relationships with Chinese officials, Huobi appears to have come under intense regulatory scrutiny in recent months. In November and December, two of the exchange's top executives were detained on suspicion of using Huobi's OTC trading services to launder money.

The matter is also "politically delicate," according to a recent Coindesk storey. To learn more, go to https://www.coindesk.com/huobi-executive-otc-custody. While this is unlikely to have any effect on the Huobi Group's cryptocurrency exchanges throughout the world, it may throw a kink in Huobi's intentions to launch a compliant DeFi ecosystem in China. Any unfavorable news regarding Huobi will depress the price of the Huobi token, just like it did in the autumn, and I have a feeling Huobi's OTC inquiry may generate a few more painful headlines before it is addressed. In comparison, I've only heard positive things about the FTX exchange in the news. FTX is a cryptocurrency derivatives exchange "created by traders for traders." Derivatives are simply instruments whose value is derived from other assets. Options and futures are examples of derivatives. Alameda Research, a cryptocurrency trading business formed by veteran Wall Street trader Sam Bankman-Freed, incubated FTX in 2019. Sam is the CEO of the FTX exchange and is well-known in the bitcoin field for his involvement. FTX, like the other crypto exchanges discussed thus far, is based in the Caribbean, namely Antigua and Barbuda. By trading volume, FTX is now the fourth largest derivatives exchange.

FTX has more than seven times the number of traded assets as Binance and Huobis, although processing only a fraction of the volume. Many of FTX's futures markets are one-of-a-kind, allowing you to trade equities before they become public and benefit when altcoins decrease using FTX's Index token. When trading these futures contracts, FTX's FTT token can be utilized as collateral. While FTX does not have a native DeFi ecosystem, FTT token holders were given SRM as a way to encourage them to utilize the serum DEX, which is based on the Solana blockchain. FTT investors can also receive reductions on trading expenses of up to 60%, as well as a portion of any surplus money in FTX's insurance fund. This insurance fund was established to reduce clawbacks. A clawback occurs when profitable traders are required to return a portion of their earnings in order for the exchange to stay viable during periods of significant market volatility. These are only a few of the advantages conferred by the FTT token. The FTT token is an ERC20 token. Despite the lack of an ICO, little over 73 million FTT were sold to private investors in three rounds at prices ranging from 10 cents to 80 cents per FTT.

These sales totaled around $10 million and amounted for little under 20% of FTT's first supply of 350 million. 175 million FTT were granted to FTX with a three-year vesting period, while the remaining 100 million FTT were dedicated to different FTX platform projects such as liquidity for FTT trading pairs. Some of the remaining FTT tokens appear to have been distributed to the FTX team and firm as well. This is presumably in addition to the 175 million. However, this lopsided allocation is irrelevant because FTT has a more aggressive repurchase and burn schedule than any other exchange token on the crypto market. The weekly buybacks and burns of the FTT token account for 33% of all trading costs on FTX. This is in addition to the 10% contribution to the insurance fund and the 5% contribution to all other FTX expenses. So far, 10 million FTT have been burnt, which is rather significant given how fresh FTX is in comparison to other crypto exchanges. On that point, FTT is one of the few exchange tokens with abundant liquidity on other respected exchanges, such as Binance, which bought a stake in FTX in December 2019. Although the dollar value of this investment was not disclosed, it is probable that it included the purchase of the 10 million FTT presently visible on the Binance chain.

The fact that the FTT token has a lot of volume on other exchanges improves the possibility that the price isn't being influenced by FTX, as it appears to be the case with many other exchange tokens. In terms of pricing, FTT has tripled since the beginning of 2022 and is now the third largest exchange token by market cap. Given that it is now ranked 40th by market cap overall, it has a lot of opportunities to expand, as does the FTX exchange. The only issue is that not everyone trades derivatives and futures contracts. Amateur traders new to the cryptocurrency industry already face a steep learning curve. FTX has done an excellent job of getting itself into the news. This is due to the revolutionary new goods and markets that they produce virtually regularly. Many of these marketplaces are luring traders from other exchanges to FTX. Most significantly, the FTT token provides significant usefulness that is not dependent on Ethereum, has excessive gas fees, or is subject to price manipulation by the exchanges that issued it. For these reasons, I believe FTT is the superior of the three exchange tokens discussed in this chapter. Other exchange tokens exist, but many aren't worth considering, and some exchanges are uncomfortably open about how they affect the price of their tokens. While exchange tokens appear to be sweeping the crypto market, keep in mind that they are essentially linked to their parent exchanges. If Binance, Huobi, or FTX have serious problems or even shut down, BNB, the Huobi Token, or FTT will all become worthless instantly. On the plus side, this reliance means there's no purpose in withdrawing tokens from exchanges for safekeeping. Remember the golden rule when it comes to your other cryptocurrencies: "not your keys, not your crypto." When not trading, keep your funds in your own wallet.

CHAPTER 11:

HOW MUCH SHOULD YOU INVEST IN BITCOIN VS ETHEREUM

Which has the most potential? What's better, Bitcoin or Ethereum? I'm not a big fan of this question since I see them as serving fundamentally distinct functions. But it's an essential question that I'm sure many of you have. It's especially important for individuals who are new to cryptocurrency and want to maximize their profits, which is precisely what I'll go over in this chapter. I'm going to look at the price potential of BTC and Eth in the short to medium term. I'll be delving into market dynamics, protocol updates, and fundamental alterations. All of this is to get to the bottom of this vexing subject. Let's begin with some pricing analysis. Bitcoin and Ethereum have both seen significant advances in recent months.

They've both surpassed their prior all-time highs during the 2017 bull run. The main difference is that Bitcoin went over its previous all-time high (ATH) in December of last year, whilst Eth only did so in early February. Furthermore, the experience for BTC and Eth has altered since then. Bitcoin's parabolic surge has continued, and it is now more than 198 percent higher than its previous all-time high. Ether, on the other hand, has experienced a more steady rise and is now just 49 percent over its previous high.

This is significant for several reasons. To begin, keep in mind that profit taking will occur. While some investors choose to sit for the long term, many others want to benefit tactically at certain levels. While virtually all Bitcoin and Ethereum wallets are profitable, Bitcoin wallets have a higher unrealized profit than

Ethereum wallets. You can validate this by looking at a number of these indicators on glassnode.com. As a result, Bitcoin hodlers are more likely to benefit at current prices than Ethereum hodlers. As we all know, when there is profit taking, it can lead to selling pressure. It's also critical to consider the market psychology of these comparable levels. If you were a novice investor, and you had to select between two distinct investments, the one that is 30 points over its ATH looks to be comparatively inexpensive in comparison to the one that is above 190 points.

While this is a simple perspective of value, it is how many new investors are likely to interpret the market. One may be considered overpriced based on historical levels, thus this newcomer purchasing pressure is more likely to be Eth-centric. That's relative past value; now consider relative worth over space. Bitcoin domination is one of the most essential measures evaluated by market experts. This is a measure of the proportion of the total crypto market cap that is occupied by Bitcoin. When BTC dominance declines, it indicates a general market shift away from Bitcoin and toward altcoins, sometimes known informally as old season. In terms of Bitcoin dominance in recent months, there has been a steady decline since December. Today, we dropped from well over 72 percent to 60 percent. Over the last two months, altcoin currency performance has been significantly greater than Bitcoin coin performance, as investors have begun to dip their toes into these waters. Despite the fact that this supremacy has been declining, we cannot deny the reality that Alts do follow Bitcoin.

They will follow if Bitcoin is on a roll. This is due to the fact that Bitcoin and altcoins are highly connected. They move together statistically. Ether, being the largest altcoin in the space, is also vulnerable to this. Any indication of a decrease in the correlation between BTC and Eth would be a positive indicator. It might imply that Ether is separating from Bitcoin. How does the correlation look? The correlation, on the other hand, has been steadily declining over the last year. It was at 90 percent in May of last year and has since dropped to an all-time low of barely 60 percent, indicating that Eth is steadily decoupling from Bitcoin. It's still a positive connection, and Eth is likely to take some signals from the Bitcoin price, but it's nowhere like as strong as it was less than a year ago. Let's put it all together: Eth is cheaper than Bitcoin based on its ATH. Unrealized profit is lower in Eth addresses than in Bitcoin addresses. Newcomers, whether or incorrectly, are more prone to believe there is more promise. We appear to be shifting to altcoins, and Eth appears to be separating from BTC. From a purely market standpoint, it appears that Eth has greater short- to medium-term upside potential. However, markets are only one factor to consider. We need to look more closely at the investor profiles of both cryptocurrencies. The large-scale mass institutional adoption of Bitcoin by institutional investors, ranging from hedge funds to company mutual funds to high net worth individuals, has been the prevailing trend throughout the last year. They've been snatching Bitcoin like it's nobody's business. The adoption trend has just recently accelerated. Indeed, the enormous increase in BTC since then has been almost entirely driven by this investor class.

The most pressing question is whether these institutional participants are also thinking about ethics. Are they wanting to diversify their Bitcoin holdings while benefiting from the leading developers of blockchain? There are several things we may look at to gain a feel of this. The quantity of Eth held by the Grayscale Investment Trust is one of the go-to measures that most analysts look at. Grayscale is the world's largest crypto trust firm, providing a wide range of funds. Up until December of last year, the total quantity of Eth held in the Grayscale Investment trust was constantly rising, but on December 8th, Grayscale called a halt to the transactions. Then, on February 1st, they reopened the gates, and the cash poured in. They acquired a total of 52,000 Eth on the first day of accepting new cash, and the trend has only gone in one direction ever then. Since February 1st, the amount of Eth owned in the Grayscale Eth fund has climbed by nearly 7% to 3.1 million. Let's also take a look at the Bitcoin trust holdings for comparison.

It grew from around 648K BTC to 655K BTC today - a 1% raise, and it isn't simply into Grayscale items. In fact, according to a Coin Shares study, inflows into Eth products accounted for a whopping 80% of all crypto fund inflows in the first two weeks of February. "We believe investors are wanting to diversify and are becoming increasingly comfortable with Ethereum fundamentals," they said. It's also worth noting that this corresponded with the launch of Eth CME futures on February 8th. Many were concerned that this would result in a similar experience to Bitcoin's price after the BTC CME futures introduction in 2017, however, the reaction was the reverse. In the first week of Eth CME futures, both open interest and volume increased steadily. Institutional investors were flocking to the futures market in droves, indicating that these investors are beginning to flip.

While they will undoubtedly continue to maintain Bitcoin as their principal asset, they are trying to diversify into altcoins, notably Ether. If the institutional enthusiasm that we've seen in the Bitcoin markets over the last four months plays out in the Eth markets, the price of Eth might explode. There are still seas of wealth in fiat land that are likely to want to invest in Bitcoin initially, however, and this is critical, It is far simpler to persuade an institution that has previously purchased Bitcoin to purchase Eth than it is to persuade a fiat-only no coiner fund to purchase their first Bitcoin. It's evident that Eth is positioned for substantial institutional investor demand, but there's another side to this demand equation to consider: utility or network demand. What motivates you to purchase Bitcoin? I'm confident the great majority of you did it to either build or protect your money from inflation.

This is, indeed, the exact argument employed by all of the institutional investors I just mentioned. Bitcoin is seen as a kind of value storage. A digital gold that funds will purchase and take to cold storage, where they will be huddled long and hard. Some may utilize it as a medium of exchange, but it is no longer regarded as the digital currency that it once was. As a result, the utility demand for Bitcoin pales in contrast to the investment desire. Ethereum, on the other hand, is a completely different kettle of fish. The Ethereum network has witnessed a surge in demand as a developer blockchain.

This has grown more apparent in light of the exponential increase of DeFi in the last year. Indeed, the unsustainable gas costs that we're now witnessing on the Ethereum network illustrate how much network demand there is. The ecosystem is in full swing, with everything from stable currencies to lending protocols and decentralized exchanges. Transaction volume has been steadily increasing over the last year and is now at an all-time high. All of the increased network usages, of course, leads to an increase in demand for Eth. Not only is Ethereum frequently utilized as collateral in many of these protocols, but also gas fees are paid in Ethereum.

As we all know, gas prices have lately skyrocketed, and I don't see this trend changing anytime soon. DeFi is heating up, and stable coin demand is skyrocketing. There are rival blockchains and companies attempting to capitalize on Eth congestion, but Eth 2.0 is being developed at a breakneck rate. We also have EIP 1559 implementation, which might deliver more predictable fees to the Ethereum network. If Eth 2.0 lives up to the hype, it has the potential to be the worldwide decentralized computer that it was envisioned to be. When it comes to Bitcoin, I don't believe we'll see any more utility demand very soon. The Taproot upgrade may bring additional smart contract capabilities to the Bitcoin blockchain, but it will be rather basic in comparison to the functionality on Ethereum. From a demand standpoint, Bitcoin looks to be utilized primarily as an investment, but Ether appears to be driven not just by rising investment demand, but also by widespread utility demand. Utility demand shows no signs of diminishing, and as we all know, with a steady supply, greater demand implies higher prices. However, that assumption is predicated on the concept of stable supply, which is far from the case. The supply cap of 21 million Bitcoins is one of the key reasons why some believe the Bitcoin supply schedule is more advantageous than Ether's. They claim that because the Ethereum network lacks a maximum supply, inflation is expected to put downward pressure on the price of Eth.

The only difficulty with this very basic analysis is that it fails to take into account the idea of sellable supply. Although Bitcoin has a protocol-defined limit and Eth does not, the price today will be influenced by the amount of supply on the market. Those coins have the potential to be sold. Both Bitcoin and Ether have suffered a persistent drop in supply on exchanges; however, in the case of Bitcoin, the drop has been around 15% since August of last year, whereas Eth has been 20%. What is the significance of this? If there is less supply on the exchanges, it indicates that there are fewer coins available to sell, which affects the price. The cryptocurrency removed from the exchange will most likely be kept in cold storage or utilized as a network utility. However, there is one significant difference between this off-exchange supply of Bitcoin and Ethereum, and that is how simple it is for that supply to return to the exchange. In the case of Bitcoin, all that is necessary is for those hodlers to get access to their cold storage and transfer the cashback to the exchange. There are no impediments to selling their coins if they want to profit. However, Ether supply is far less flexible due to two major factors: Ether locked in smart contracts and Ether staked in the Eth 2.0 deposit contract. Let's begin with the first. As previously stated, there is a tremendous need for Ether to be utilized in DeFi protocols. This Ether is frequently used as collateral in smart contracts and protocols, where it yields a return.

Let us now look at those monies. The total value locked TVL is at an all-time high, having risen from 15 billion at the start of the year to about 40 billion at the time of writing this book. So, if you've locked your Eth in a smart contract and it's generating you a reasonable dividend, there's a stronger disincentive to release it and sell it. However, there is one Eth smart contract that takes the sticky notion to a whole new level. This is due to the fact that the

Ether held in this smart contract cannot be removed anytime soon. I'm referring to the Eth 2.0 staking contract. This is the beacon chain contract where Eth holders may stake their Eth to gain staking incentives.

However, unlike other DeFi protocols, Eth locked in the staking contract cannot yet be withdrawn. That means that all of the Ether being delivered here will not be able to be returned to the market very soon. Currently, more than 3.2 million Eth are locked in the deposit contract. Since the contract's inception last year, this has grown at a constant and regular rate. This tendency likewise appears to be showing no signs of abating. We presently have approximately 3.2 million Eth removed from the market for the time being. That is not going to contribute to any form of selling pressure any time soon. If you go to glassnode, you can see the proportion of total Ether supply that is now held in smart contracts. We increased from a little over 10% in July 2020 to over 20% by March 2022.

From a supply standpoint, it appears that Eth is in a better position. But there is one more supply element that we must discuss. One that will put an end to the idea that Ethereum is an inflationary asset. EIP 1559, along with Eth 2.0, is one of the hottest topics in the Ethereum community right now. It's an Ethereum enhancement proposal that would alter how users bid for transactions to be included in blocks. This update would essentially set a market rate for the gas charge necessary for block inclusion.

This is referred to as the base charge. Users can still pay the mining as a tip if they wish to complete their transaction more faster. What are the key advantages of this? Contrary to common belief, it will not cut gas prices. What it does, though, is make gas fee management much more predictable. It is critical to clarify this. However, hodlers are primarily interested in what this EIP impacts to the Ether supply. This is due to the fact that it will ensure that the aforementioned basic charge is burned, destroyed, and removed from circulation. Given that gas is paid in Eth, it follows that Eth will be burnt; hence, the more the Ethereum network is utilized, the more Ether will be burned and removed from the supply.

When network use is at an all-time high, it signifies that a lot of Eth will be burned. In fact, if network use is widespread, the burn rate may be able to nearly totally neutralize the inflationary component. This means that, in theory, Eth may face the same long-term scarcity argument as Bitcoin. Instead of a protocol-defined limit, you get excessive network use and Eth burns. It's time to call it a day. When it comes to the debate between Bitcoin and Ethereum, I believe I can approach it objectively. In the near to medium term, it appears that Eth has the upper hand. Its price is lower in comparison to its ATH, and new investors are aware of this. I've also discussed how institutional investors are beginning to shift their focus to altcoins, but it's not a huge leap of faith to dedicate a portion of your institutional portfolio to Eth if you already own Bitcoin. Then, of course, there's the massive utility demand on the Ethereum network right now. Regardless of how innovative Bitcoin is, its use as a medium of commerce is declining. It's an asset owned for investment purposes, and that isn't going to change anytime soon. Finally, the Eth market supply deficit is anticipated to have a long-term influence on the price. It's trapped in smart contracts and can't be readily traded, and we can't forget about the forthcoming EIP update, which might potentially erase any network inflation. It has the potential to make that rare digital platinum as valuable as Bitcoin's gold. Of course, there are always hazards in this situation.

The gas taxes are debilitating, forcing consumers to other ecosystems. You should also keep in mind that miners are not lovers of EIP1559, and Eth 2.0 may be postponed again. Perhaps there will be a fresh wave of institutional Bitcoin purchases from an unexpected source. However, on the balance of probabilities, I believe that Eth will outperform in the next months. You're undoubtedly wondering where the price is heading now. On the Bitcoin front, I believe we will be well on our way to the $100,000 mark before the end of the summer. This is the level at which the stock expects to flow, and it has recently done an excellent job of charting that price. You should also consider Biden's 1.5 trillion dollar stimulus, which is expected to flood retail money into crypto. It's highly possible that Bitcoin may reach $150,000 before the end of the year, given similar divergences as witnessed in prior bull cycles. EIP 1559 is set to be released in July on Ethereum. The enthusiasm around this upgrade may cause the price to rise over $5,000 when fee burns begin to take effect and we get closer to the next stage of Eth 2.0. This enthusiasm might propel Eth over $10,000 by the end of 2022. Those are my predictions, but they are only my opinion, and I am not a financial advisor, so take them with a grain of salt.

CHAPTER 12:

WHAT PRIVACY COINS YOU MUST INVEST

Cryptocurrencies did, at one point, protect your privacy. This was due to the fact that, despite the fact that blockchains such as Bitcoin and Ethereum are public, it was difficult, if not impossible, to link transactions to individual identities. Anyone can now launch a blockchain explorer and discover which wallets contain certain coins. There are also specialist blockchain research organizations, such as Chainalysis, that are always on the alert for nefarious behavior. As a result, maintaining your anonymity in the crypto ecosystem is becoming more difficult, and it doesn't help that authorities are forcing exchanges to delist privacy currencies like Monero. But I think that privacy is a human right, and I know there must be a method to safeguard it on the blockchain without inviting the ban hammer, and it just so happens that two cryptocurrency initiatives have done precisely that. Secret Network and Tornado Cash have developed a solution to give complete anonymity while being compliant.

Both of their tokens have witnessed amazing development thus far, and in this chapter, I'll explain why the best is yet to come. Secret Network's origins begin with another cryptocurrency project named Enigma. Enigma, which debuted in 2014, was a layer 2 scaling solution for Ethereum that included privacy-preserving smart contracts. After a community vote a few months later, Enigma opened its primary net in February 2020 and was renamed to Secret Network. However, calling Secret Network a continuation of Enigma isn't fully correct. This is due to the fact that Enigma MPC, the company that created Enigma, is now simply one of several firms working on Secret Network. Tor Bear, Enigma's previous head of growth and marketing, is also the creator of Secret Network.

Secret Network is the first cryptocurrency network to enable Secret Contracts, which are privacy-preserving smart contracts. Any transactions done within Secret Contracts are entirely concealed from everyone, including the Secret Network blockchain's validator nodes. However, the native SCRT token of Secret Network is not a privacy coin. In reality, like BTC and Eth, all SCRT transactions are public.

What is the source of privacy?

Secret Tokens are the answer. Secret Tokens are the assets utilized in Secret Contracts on the Secret Network. These cryptocurrencies, like Monero and Grin, maintain anonymity by default. Secret token holders have access to a viewing key, which they may use to confirm their ownership of whatever assets they have in Secret Contracts, in order to guarantee regulatory compliance. Secret Network's combination of anonymity and transparency enables it to meet a wide range of use cases that other cryptocurrency blockchains cannot, such as DeFi applications that are immune to front-running. Rather than directly competing with other smart contract blockchains, Secret Network aspires to be the privacy center for the whole cryptocurrency ecosystem. What precisely is the Secret Network? Secret Network was created with the Cosmos SDK. Tendermint, a Byzantine fault tolerant delegated proof-of-stake consensus technique, is used. This indicates that Secret Network may theoretically process between 10 and 14,000 transactions per second, while no official statistic is available at this time. As a result, Secret Network is considerably less decentralized, with a maximum of 50 validator nodes at any given moment. In contrast to many other Tendermint networks, validators on the Secret Network can have their stakes reduced for downtime and can even be blacklisted if they attempt to influence transactions.

These secret validators are also in charge of the Secret Contracts. Secret Network contracts achieve anonymity by executing inside trusted execution environments, or TEES. TEES are utilized in a variety of applications ranging from video games to cellphones. They act as a black box, allowing computations to be done over encrypted data. Secret Tokens used in Secret Contracts are created following the Snip 20 standard, which is similar to Ethereum's ERC20 standard. Secret Tokens are created by depositing ordinary assets, such as the SCRT token, into a smart contract.

When utilizing Secret Tokens, all account balances, transactions, and transaction amounts are kept confidential, and secret SCRT is only one of several Secret Tokens you may create. As of mid-March 2022, you may manufacture over 20 Ethereum tokens as Secret Tokens on the Secret Network, utilizing the Secret Ethereum Bridge, which supports Eth and USDC. The Secret Ethereum Bridge is also bidirectional, which means you may use SCRT as a wrapped ERC20 token on Ethereum. When you consider the coin's tokenomic history, this is quite amusing. The SCRT currency did not have an ICO. Enigma token holders were instead offered the option of burning ENG on Ethereum to generate an equivalent quantity of SCRT on the Secret Network. ENG was still listed on Binance at the moment, which indicated in October that they would facilitate the switch of ENG to SCRT. Before the convertibility period ended on January 1st, 2022, around 115 million ENG were burnt. This procedure resulted in a wonderfully fair allocation of SCRT, which is exactly what you want given that the coin is also used to table and vote on Secret Network proposals.

However, Secret Network revised its tokenomics in December 2020, revealing that it issued around 50 million extra coins to finance various activities. These distributions are a little strange, given that the hidden foundation receives 15% of all staking winnings as part of a foundation tax intended to encourage network growth. On the plus side, a quick look at the SCRT balances on one of Secret Network's block explorers indicates that the currency distribution is still pretty equitable. Wallets are also identified on this block explorer, which is unusual for younger coins. SCRT has a current supply of around 177 million units and an annual inflation rate of 15%. This inflation is used to compensate validators and delegators by 26 and 28 percent per year, respectively. 44 percent of the supply is now staked, with the majority of this coming from the current circulating supply of 70 million.

This is essential since any staked SCRT has a 21-day unlocking period, which means it won't be appearing on any exchanges very soon if the price begins to rise. In terms of price activity, SCRT has pulled a 5x since the beginning of the year and is still in an obvious uptrend. Given that Secret Network has a market capitalization of less than $200 million dollars and no prior opposition, there is still plenty of space for growth. Unfortunately, it does not have a high trading volume, and Binance is the only respectable exchange that handles it. This is hardly surprising given the massive quantity of SCRT that is now staked. If you want to stake or receive liquidity mining rewards for the hidden Ethereum bridge, you may do it easily with the Kepler wallet browser plugin. To engage with Secret

Network's forthcoming DAPps, you'll also need the Kepler wallet. Aside from the secret Ethereum Bridge, Secret Network has just developed the world's first privacy-preserving DEX. SecretSwap is modeled after AMMs like Uniswap and SushiSwap, and like these two, it will have its own governance token. They have only referred to it as Gov tokens, but additional details should be available in the coming months. Whereas SCRT is used to vote on Secret Network modifications, this DeFi Gov token will allow holders to not only adjust SecretSwaps specifications but also influence the direction of the Secret Network's whole DeFi ecosystem. While SecretSwap and the Secret Ethereum Bridge are presently the sole DeFi protocols on Secret Network, Secret Network just announced DeFi ecosystem grants. Secret Network already has a lengthy list of requested DeFi protocols, such as synthetic assets, lending, borrowing, and automatic yield protocols such as Yearn Finance. If

Binance's financing of its own DeFi technologies is any indication, Secret Network might see some spectacular TVL stats. The Secret Ethereum Bridge already has over $50 million in Ethereum assets locked up, which represents more than a fourth of the SCRT coin's market valuation. Secret Network also has a significant advantage over other wannabe DeFi ecosystems in that it has Gamified network expansion through the usage of Secret Network Committees.

These Secret Network Committees are made up of "secret agents" who get 2% of all staking rewards in exchange for helping to improve and grow the Secret Network's reach. This is comparable to Kusama's Kappa Sigma Mu organization, but with more concrete and significant objectives. Despite the rather dubious tokenomics around allocation, Secret Network appears to be on track for significant growth in 2022, as does Tornado Cash. Tornado Cash was created in August 2019 by quantum statistician Roman Semionov and Roman Storm. For years, the two Romans have been involved in the cryptocurrency industry, focusing on layer 2 scaling solutions for Ethereum and privacy technologies like ZK Snarks.

They attend cryptocurrency hackathons on a regular basis, and Roman Semionov indicated in an interview that they attempt to attend as many as possible. In 2018, they established Pepesec, a software firm that creates DAPps and offers smart auditing services. Tornado Cash is a protocol that allows private transactions to be sent on Ethereum. Ethereum is a blockchain that is open to the public. This means you can watch every Ethereum transaction as it happens. You can see who is delivering the asset, who is getting it, how much they paid for petrol, and so on. Prior to Tornado Cash, there were various privacy-preserving protocols for Ethereum, but none had succeeded in breaking the connection between the sender and the receiver in an Ethereum transaction. Tornado Cash has gotten no venture capital financing and just a few tiny community donations through Molok Dao and other similar crypto crowdfunding sites. Tornado cache allows you to transmit Eth, USDC, and USDT to any Ethereum address in secret. You can even transmit these assets to a fresh Ethereum address with a 0 balance. This is crucial because, in order to claim assets from an Ethereum protocol, you must normally pay gas costs in Eth.

Tornado Cash circumvents this need, and here's how. Tornado cash pushes cryptocurrency mixing to new heights. Assume you have a bag of coins. Anyone is welcome to deposit their money into the bag. Assume you put five coins in the bag. When you do this, you'll be handed a notice stating that you may claim five coins whenever you like. Assuming that enough individuals have tossed their money into the bag, the five coins you pull out when you utilize that receipt will not be the initial coins you tossed in. This disconnects the coins you put from the ones you remove. This is similar to how Tornado Cash operates, except that everything takes place on Ethereum. Instead of putting money in a bag, they go into a smart contract, and instead of a receipt, you get cryptographic proof. ZK Snarks, a privacy mechanism employed in Zcash, allows you to claim your coins using the proof without exposing which coins you first put to receive that proof, thereby severing the link between sender and recipient. You may utilize one of Tornado Cash's dozen or so relayers to move Ethereum assets to a fresh new address with no Eth to cover withdrawal costs. These relayers, in effect, submit the cryptographic evidence on your behalf. All you have to do is send it together with the new Ethereum address.

You'll need some more Eth for the withdrawal, as well as a modest charge for their service, and you'll have an anonymous Ethereum wallet. Furthermore, the relays never truly get possession of your assets. They can only transmit funds from the smart contract to the Ethereum address you provided. This is ensured by the protocol's code. While this technology is extremely strong, it does have certain drawbacks. Because a smart contract is required for each asset and denomination, the size and privacy of each transaction are restricted by the number of persons depositing into that specific smart contract. For example, suppose 10,000 individuals have deposited into the smart contract for 10 Eth, but less than 200 people have invested into the smart contract for 1,000 DAI, and there appear to be no or insufficient participants to operate the 10K and 100K DAI smart contracts.

There are also certain other privacy precautions you should take while moving cash to avoid being traced in other ways. You should be aware that Tornado Cash complies with all legislation. If necessary, anybody can use their cryptographic proof to demonstrate the link between the funds they placed and the monies they withdrew. This is significant because certain exchanges will refuse to accept money from cryptocurrency blends such as Tornado Cash. Although this compliance tool allows you to deposit those mixed monies into an exchange, I doubt it will be easy to explain what's going on to an exchange's customer care representative. I also don't believe Tornado Cash's Torn cryptocurrency will be listed on any regulated exchanges anytime soon. Torn is an ERC20 token that serves as the Tornado Cash protocol's governing coin. The currency did not have an ICO; instead, vouchers to claim the tokens were airdropped to any Ethereum wallet addresses that put assets into the protocol prior to December 6, 2020. This was one of the most profitable cryptocurrency airdrops of all time, with the average consumer getting 66 Torn valued more over $23,000. In contrast to past airdrops, the amount of Torn a wallet got was less reliant on the amount of Eth deposited. This led to an extremely equal Torn distribution, which is precisely what you want for a governance token.

Torn has a maximum supply of 10 million, with around 500,000 Torn airdropped to users. Another million was put aside for anonymity mining, which compensates Torn users for depositing assets into the numerous smart contracts I discussed before. The DOW treasury has 5.5 million Torn, with the remaining 3 million earmarked for the founders and early sponsors. All of these coins have different vesting timelines. If you're wondering why Torn's price history starts at the beginning of February 2022, it's because token transfers were restricted until that point and could only be opened by a community vote. This neatly permitted the founders to avoid any regulatory attention that may have resulted from controlling the unlock.

They were also able to generate a lot of money as a result of it. When it comes to Torn's price potential, the dollar worth of assets locked is typically used to determine if an Ethereum protocol is over or undervalued. Given that Torn has a market size of roughly $100 million, the fact that there are 300 million dollars worth of assets on the protocol suggests that Torn might experience at least a threefold increase from its present pricing. The issue is that there is no way of knowing whether this TVL is organic or simply Yield farmers attempting to earn some of those anonymous mining riches. From a supply demand standpoint, there is a lot more torn that has yet to hit the market, and I'm not sure whether there is enough demand to fulfill it. However, during a bull run, this type of objective reasoning is rendered null and worthless. Torn is likely to be invested in by more than one individual. The question is whether they will be prepared to pay the Ethereum gas costs to purchase it on Uniswap given that there are currently no viable alternatives.

This is largely dependent on what Tornado Cash has in store for development, which also appears to be fairly unknown. Even though Tornado Cash appears to have a high degree of participation in governance, it's unclear how much its community can influence at the protocol level. This is due to the fact that the Romans destroyed their admin keys in May of 2020, making any changes to the protocol impossible. Some consider this approach as irresponsible since the Romans will not be able to save the day as they did previously. Others lauded the action as adhering to the Bitcoin Ethos of code being law. After all, Tornado Cash's code has been inspected several times, and the developers specialize in smart contract audits. They deleted their admin keys as a result of regulatory pressure. More than one three-letter agency is most certainly keeping tabs on the Romans.

That's a concern because they're among the few individuals who can create these complicated privacy procedures. I'd be more concerned if they hadn't disposed of the admin keys. They performed a wonderful job and even drew the notice of Vitalik Buterin, who has been an enthusiastic supporter of the initiative. I suppose all the publicity in the world can't remove the news of Tornado Cash being used to launder stolen bitcoin. These aren't the finest optics to have, especially when you're running a smart contract security firm. Tornado Cash is still a game changer in the cryptocurrency sector, and it has raised the bar for both developers and authorities.

CHAPTER 13:

WHAT ORACLE CRYPTOS YOU MUST INVEST

Did you know that an Oracle is required for more than 80% of decentralized apps in the crypto space? This should not be surprising. After all, if you want to create useful DAPps based on real-world use cases, you'll need valuable real-world data. Data such as asset prices, weather, and information on the outcomes of events such as sporting events and elections Oracles are also important in DeFi protocols, which today handle billions of dollars in user payments. Because of this Oracle reliance, many claims that Oracle cryptos are among the most valuable on the crypto market.

The current market leader in the Oracle field is, of course, ChainLink, although the Link token appears to be losing ground versus Bitcoin. What may be causing this lackluster price movement? Is this an indication that ChainLink's finest days are behind it, or is it a hint that Link is about to rocket to new all-time highs? In this chapter, I'll address all of those questions and more. Steve Ellis and Sergey Nazarov created ChainLink in June 2017. Both are also the creators of smart contract, a San Francisco-based software startup that is developing the ChainLink ecosystem. Having stated that, ChainLink is formally incorporated as a smart contract ChainLink Limited SEZC in the Cayman Islands. ChainLink seeks to overcome the Oracle problem in cryptocurrencies. The Oracle issue is truly twofold. First, cryptocurrency blockchains are by nature unable to access external data, and second, employing any centralized data feeds would undermine the decentralization of the smart contract or application using the data feed since it would have a single centralized point of failure. Naturally, the solution to this problem is a decentralized data set provided by hundreds of trusted entities who are given economic incentives to collect their data when a smart contract requests it. ChainLink is essentially what it is. It acts as a bridge between real-world data and data stored on cryptocurrency blockchains.

As a result, ChainLink incorporates both off-chain and on-chain components. ChainLink is an off-chain community of Oracle nodes that link to cryptocurrency blockchains such as Ethereum. ChainLink is a set of smart contracts that allow developers to request data for their DAPps from the aforementioned Oracle nodes on-chain, especially on Ethereum. The Link token is used to pay Oracle nodes for data feeds and will ultimately be used for staking by Oracle nodes to ensure they consistently supply high-quality data feeds. Each data stream has dozens of Oracle nodes, and developers can utilize one or more nodes based on their own preferences or the competitive pricing supplied by nodes through their bidding process.

The ChainLink mainnet went operational in May 2019, less than two years after its initial coin offering (ICO) in September 2017 garnered a comfortable 32 million dollars in Eth. ChainLink's ecosystem has grown rapidly since then, as has the value of the Link token. ChainLink now delivers 75 price feeds to over 300 bitcoin smart contracts and decentralized apps. But this only scratches the surface of what ChainLink has done, and the majority of these successes have occurred in the previous few months. ChainLink will launch its community awards program in August 2020. This effort aims to accelerate the expansion of ChainLink's ecosystem. ChainLink has since supported 19 separate research and development awards. Notable grants include those for native ChainLink integration on Tezos, Solana, and Avalanche. ChainLink even offered LinkMarine a grant to construct and operate a website for ChainLink-related news. According to my knowledge, this is the first time ChainLink has funded a LinkMarine.

The link was introduced as a collateral option to produce the DAI stable coin in Maker DAO in September 2020, giving the token additional use. But it wasn't until October 2020 that things really started to pick up for ChainLink. To begin, BitGo, the business that issues wBTC, the biggest wrapped Bitcoin token on Ethereum, has teamed up with ChainLink to provide proof of reserves. This implies that consumers may be certain that the wBTC in circulation on the Ethereum blockchain is backed up one to one by the Bitcoin in BitGo's custody.

ChainLink introduced a new product named ChainLink VRF towards the end of October. VRF is an abbreviation for verified random function, which is necessary for RNG, or Random Number Generation, which is commonly used in video games. ChainLink now provides on-chain VRF and off-chain VRF offered by Oracle nodes to developers developing Ethereum gaming DAPps. Prior to ChainLink's VRF, RNG did not exist on Ethereum, marking a significant milestone not only for ChainLink but for the whole Ethereum ecosystem. The introduction of the Trust token, the business that produces the TUSD stablecoin that will use ChainLink for proof of reserves, in November sustained ChainLink's milestone momentum.

On ChainLink's dedicated data feeds website, you can now quickly verify whether there is enough USD backing the TUSD in circulation. Soon after, it was stated that Matic was the first cryptocurrency blockchain, other than Ethereum, to natively incorporate ChainLink's data feeds. The cryptocurrency community was pleading for ChainLink at the end of November, but not because of its bombardment of positive news. In October and November, a half-dozen DeFi protocols, including Compound Finance, Harvest Finance, and Acropolis, were all targeted by flash loan assaults. Over a hundred million dollars in bitcoin was lost. It is not totally correct to refer to these large-scale arbitrage trades as assaults. This is due to the fact that it simply requires taking advantage of pricing variations between various DeFi protocols.

Typically, this entails borrowing millions of dollars worth of one cryptocurrency on one DEX with a flashlight, selling that cryptocurrency at a profit on another DEX, repaying the flashlight, and retaining the difference. The issue is that these big lighting swaps don't bode well for the DeFi space. When ordinary investors and institutions see a headline stating that Compound Finance would lose 90 million dollars, I doubt they will be interested in participating. According to AAve creator Stani Kolechov, if we want to see substantial DeFi adoption, we must assess and reduce this risk.

This is when ChainLink enters the picture. More often than not, the ability to conduct these enormous arbitrage deals is due to reliance on centralized price feeds, rather than a problem with the protocols involved. In brief, many of the DeFi protocols that are targeted by flashlight attacks rely on pricing data from a single DEX, such as Uniswap, making them open to price manipulation flaws. Fortunately, the remedy is straightforward. To avoid these terrifying multi-million dollar arbitrage DeFi transactions, use an Oracle like ChainLink to collect pricing data from several DEXs and other sources. To defend themselves from DeFiDegens, many of DeFi protocols have subsequently included ChainLink and other pricing Oracles. Many people consider ChainLink to be a hero as a result of this, yet there are many who believe he is a villain in disguise. Of course, I'm referring to Zeus Capital.

In November 2020, Zeus Capital offered a $100,000 reward to anyone who could supply them with information on ChainLink's illegal and deceptive tactics. Why? Because they are putting together a class-action lawsuit against ChainLink, probably for the losses they received when they shorted Link earlier in 2020. As many LinkMarines are aware, Zeus Capital has shorted Link because, in their opinion, ChainLink is a big ponzi scam and the Link token will soon be worthless. One week later, Zeus Capital said that the Link token will be classed as a security by the SEC in the United States. If this is accurate, it means that ChainLink will be treated similarly to Ripple, and the Link token will be delisted from US exchanges and dumped by any significant institutional investors based in the US, just as XRP was. You may dismiss this as another senseless FUD from Zeus Capital, but I believe it is worth considering given that the SEC is looking at other cryptocurrency projects outside Ripple.

There is no way to predict if ChainLink will be investigated by the SEC. This is due to a variety of factors. First, while ChainLink is established in the Cayman Islands, it is unclear whether smart contract, the firm behind ChainLink, is incorporated in the United States. If this is the case, the project may be inside the SEC's firing range. Second, because all monies were gathered in Eth, it appears that there were no limits on who may participate in the ChainLink ICO. If anybody in the United States is determined to have participated in the ChainLink ICO, Link may be subject to SEC oversight. However, even if Link is subject to SEC scrutiny, that does not automatically make Link a security.

This is assessed using a procedure known as the "howey test." The TLDR on whether or not Link is a security boils down to whether or not the token's price action is based on the activities of a third party, in this instance ChainLink. Given that Link has actual use as a way of payment for Oracle services, establishing causation is difficult. When staking becomes available, it will give a new level of price effect to the Linked token. This, I believe, is why the Crypto Ratings Council gave ChainLink a two-out-of-five grade for how closely it fits the parameters of the Howey test. Given that the Crypto Ratings Council granted XRP a four out of five, I believe we are secure from the SEC. However, I believe that additional lawsuits against ChainLink from inside the bitcoin industry will be filed in the coming months. Why? In early December 2020, ChainLink and the World Economic Forum published a whitepaper outlining criteria for decentralized Oracles. What is the issue here? Aside from the fact that the World Economic Forum isn't exactly concerned with the common person's best interests, the document was produced by ChainLink founder Sergey Nazarov, and the Oracle standards he outlines are those utilized by ChainLink. To put it another way, ChainLink is the industry standard. Competing Oracles, such as band protocol, do not fulfill the criterion and should thus be barred from working with public and private entities. API3 was scheduled to organize a hackathon at Eth India online and Etherpunk 2022 in late December, however, they were notified that ChainLink had purchased the rights to function as the exclusive Oracle supplier for the aforementioned events. API3 is effectively barred from participating in any way. In a blog post, API3 admits that both event organizers have the right to grant this type of exclusive access, but it still reveals monopolistic practices by ChainLink, which are not limited to events like hackathons and even extend to some smart contract platforms as rights to employ and or promote Oracle services competing with the interests of the party proposing such agreements, in exchange for financial compensation. Given that API3 has publicly said that it is a ChainLink killer, I believe there is enough prejudice on their end.

This type of anticompetitive action, however, is not unusual in the crypto sector, and I would not rule out any enterprise, including ChainLink, engaging in it. If objective proof emerges that ChainLink has been engaging in such dubious behavior, we may begin to see a legal backlash from competitors in the crypto market. Although I cannot tell for definite what happened or did not happen at these hackathons, this alleged occurrence may help explain why ChainLink has been selling an abnormally large number of Link tokens in recent months. In September 2020, a coin telegraph headline reported, "ChainLink up 30 after six-week downturn and developer selloff." At the time, I didn't pay much attention to this report because the circulating supply of Link was still 350 million, according to CoinMarketCap. Imagine my surprise when I discovered, during my latest investigation, that the circulating supply of Link had unexpectedly increased to nearly 400 million. https://coinmarketcap.com/currencies/chainlink/ Because Link is an ERC20 token, you may use Etherscan to effortlessly follow all

Link transactions and balances. I discovered a wallet address that had recently transferred 500,000 Link every few days. According to a Glassnode Medium article from 2019, it belongs to the ChainLink team. This wallet held a balance of around 35.6 million Link at the time. Moving funds is not a smoking gun, but an in-depth report from Trust notes dated August 2020 appears to be just that. In a nutshell, it looks that the ChainLink team has sold hundreds of thousands of Link. According to the study, the ChainLink team is aggressively attempting to obscure or conceal those transactions.

According to a recent news report, the ChainLink team's selling activity is what caused Link to lose momentum in mid-August. What's the point of all this Link? Well, there are a few options. First, an item from early July 2020 mentions that ChainLink intends to invest millions in development. It states that 500,000 Link are sent twice a month to Oracle node operators, but that these Link are coming from ChainLink team wallet addresses rather than the 350 million Link war chest wallet assigned to node operator rewards. Second, remember that ChainLink has made 19 awards through its community grants program.

It just so happens that this program began on July 31, 2020. The sale of Link tokens by grant recipients is very likely one of the reasons Link's moonshot was cut short in mid-August, and why the Link token continues to struggle versus Bitcoin. Finally, LinkMarines will be aware that ChainLink appears to be Oracle Facebook's new digital currency project DM will use to guarantee its multiple tokens are appropriately pegged to the fiat assets they will represent. If this collaboration exists, something tells me it was expensive, given that the DM group has a membership price of $10 million. Furthermore, ChainLink's flirting with the World Economic Forum makes me assume that the team is eager to collaborate with both public and private entities. Perhaps this is where all of the Link from those team wallets is going, and it would also explain why ChainLink has been so secretive about how its money has been used. Typically, these private relationships are exposed considerably later in the process. Even if I'm accurate, it doesn't change the reality that millions of Links are discarded every week.

Even though I believe in ChainLink as a concept, I feel the Link token will lag during this bull market due to the team's sales of Link. Regardless of recent price activity. The issue is whether ChainLink's significant investment in growth and partnerships will pay off in the long run. Personally, I believe that it will. ChainLink has done in the last few months what other cryptocurrency initiatives have taken years to achieve. This is mostly due to ChainLink's community funding program, which appears to be in its early stages. Given the extraordinary devotion of LinkMarines, I have a feeling this community award will not be the last of its sort. Similarly, ChainLink's collaboration with Trust token might set a new standard for stable currencies in the future. I'd love for ChainLink to give proof of reserves for stable currencies like Tether, and if the market wants it, it may happen. ChainLink's growth into other cryptocurrency blockchains will also present some intriguing quandaries. Is it possible that the Link token will appear on other blockchains? I believe it is doable, and others claim that it is only a question of time. Others, on the other hand, anticipate that Link will reach zero before that day arrives. Zeus Capital appears to have paid out over $20,000 in bounty awards to whistleblowers who say that ChainLink has participated in dubious tactics, and if their case is successful, it may attract the attention of regulators such as the SEC. While I believe ChainLink is secure in that regard, the team's lack of openness over what they're doing with their Link tokens may get them in hot water. This hidden sell-off appears to have been going on for years, and ChainLink has yet to clarify where those monies are going. To be fair, this might be because they're forming the type of business ties that aren't made public until they're finalized.

I'm simply wondering if Link's price will hold up until these collaborations are exposed if they exist at all. Worse, you can't really believe the naysayers when they're all blatantly biassed against ChainLink and, in some cases, downright jealous of the project's success. Having said that, I believe it is prudent to be cautious. During this bull market, I will be keeping a careful eye on ChainLink's team wallet addresses. If you have a Link, I recommend you do the same.

CHAPTER 14:

WHAT ARE THE BEST SMART CONTRACT BLOCKCHAINS TO INVEST

Smart contracts are one of the most lucrative technologies to come from the crypto sector. Using smart contracts instead of centralized middlemen has shown to be more profitable and convenient for those who understand how to utilize them. There is one little issue: many smart contracts today are limited in their capacity to efficiently collect data from the blockchains on which they are based. This implies that if developers wish to construct a new decentralized application or improve an existing one, they will have to spend extra time and money manually gathering that data. If smart contracts and decentralized apps are to genuinely replace their centralized counterparts, a more efficient method of querying the data necessary to construct and manage them is required. The Graph aspires to be this much-needed data indexing layer.

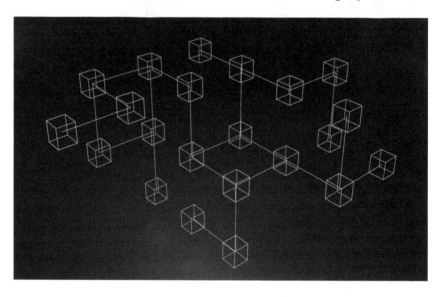

The worldwide Graph of all smart contract blockchain information. So, in this chapter, I'll explain why the Graph might be one of the most important initiatives to emerge in the cryptocurrency sector. Electrical Engineer Yaniv Tal, Computer Scientist Janis Pullman, and Robotics Brandon Ramirez established The Graph. The trio have previously collaborated on many firms that created developer tools for a variety of applications. After a while, they began to question why it was so difficult to construct developer tools, and they realized it was mostly due to a reliance on centralized databases. If you wish to create a standard application, you must utilize a database. This database is likely to be controlled by a tech behemoth such as Amazon, Facebook, Apple, or Microsoft. In addition to these corporations' bad track records with data, any modifications made to that data can have far-reaching consequences for both app developers and consumers. Because these organizations are also hesitant to publicly share the data they possess in custody, data silos form, making it extremely difficult to construct genuinely effective applications. When the three discovered Ethereum in 2017, they were enamored with its possibilities and began developing decentralized apps on the Ethereum network. However, they were soon met with another congestion. Although Ethereum has a large quantity of data that is readily accessible to developers, searching through that data is quite arduous, making it hard to design more complicated Daps without experiencing significant slowness. They decided to address this issue by developing a data indexing mechanism for Ethereum and IPFS, which would later be known as the Graph.

The project's inaugural white paper was prepared in March 2017, and the Graph was formally launched a year later in June 2018. The Graph just recently completed its ICO, and its GRT token will begin trading on major exchanges in December 2020, which surprised many. First, we must comprehend what the Graph is and how it operates. To fully grasp what the Graph is and why it is so crucial in the crypto ecosystem, we must first explore how decentralized apps function. To keep things simple, a decentralized application is made up of a collection of smart contracts that function in unison. Smart contracts are immutable programs that execute a sequence of actions or transactions automatically when a set of conditions is satisfied. Ethereum is used to build the majority of decentralized apps, which is why it is the second largest cryptocurrency by market cap. There are several types of decentralized apps, the most prominent of which are DeFi applications such as Uniswap, Maker DAO, and Aave.

A decentralized application requires data from the Ethereum blockchain in order to function. It requires data from the Ethereum blockchain, as well as a location to store any data generated by its users. Price is the most straightforward example of off-chain data. This real-world data must be loaded into the Ethereum blockchain and distributed to the decentralized application that requires price information.

This is accomplished by the use of a decentralized Oracle, such as the ChainLink or Banned protocols. Few decentralized apps would function without the real-world data given by these Oracles, which is why ChainLink is also one of the biggest cryptocurrencies by market size. Moving on, there are initiatives like Filecoin that provide decentralized data storage. Storge and other Ethereum-native decentralized data storage protocols are also available. For the time being, the majority of data created by DAPps on Ethereum is simply stored on the Ethereum blockchain, without the usage of a complex protocol. This gets us to the final jigsaw piece: data on the Ethereum blockchain. Because Ethereum is open source, you may inspect all of the code that makes up a decentralized program, as well as any data created by that decentralized application. Assume you want to create an Ethereum-based marketplace aggregate dap where users can see all the parcels of land for sale in Ethereum-based virtual worlds such as Decentraland and the Sandbox.

This would include obtaining data from each individual marketplace and incorporating it into your marketplace aggregator. Because everything on the Ethereum blockchain is open source, this would be fairly simple to implement, and the simplicity of the data being requested means it wouldn't take long for your Dap to discover it. However, say you wanted to introduce a service that allowed customers to view the selling history of each of these markets across certain time periods. After all, those who are in the business of flipping virtual land may be interested in such information.

Finding this type of particular data may take the Dap hours or even days, making it hard for land traders to receive the up-to-date information they want to conduct a good flip. As a developer, it would likewise be tough to create the code necessary to retrieve this exact data. The Graph addresses this issue by allowing developers can instantly retrieve both complicated and basic data from the Ethereum blockchain that their DAPps require. The Graph is the puzzle's third and final piece. The layer of data sorting between the blockchain and Dap. It improves the efficiency of current DAPps and makes the development of new DAPps easier. This, in turn, raises the possibility that DAPps will outperform their centralized counterparts and usher in the new age of decentralization that so many have envisioned. But how does the Graph function? The Graph, on the other hand, serves as a type of marketplace for particular data on Ethereum. Each data set on this marketplace is referred to as a Subgraph, and it may be seen using Graph Explorer. There are Subgraphs for data from DAPps such as Uniswap, Compound, USDC, and even Decentraland, as you can see. Each Subgraph is essentially a description of individual smart contracts within those DAPps, as well as any values included within them that might be important to someone establishing a new Dap utilizing that data. Consider this the equivalent of using bookmarks and a highlighter on a textbook. Every Subgraph description is copied and saved on the IPFS, Filecoin's decentralized data storage layer. A DAPp developer may quickly obtain the data that they want for their Dap utilizing the Graph explorer and the Graph's own straightforward querying language called Graphql. When a developer makes a data request, index nodes on the Graph network search across relevant Subgraphs to discover the information. Indexers decide which Subgraphs to extract data from based on what's known as a curation signal, which is given by curators who create Subgraphs and evaluate their quality. Naturally, a set of economic incentives is required for this process to succeed. As a result, everyone looking for data in the Graph Explorer must pay indexes query costs, which are established by the indexes and are charged in Eth or DAI. Indexers can also receive inflationary indexing incentives in the form of GRT tokens. Delegate a stake GRT to let the Graph protocol know which indexes to utilize to gather data for developers to guarantee that indexers do not overcharge developers for their services. Delegators are compensated a share of query fees and indexing incentives for providing this service.

Indexers must invest GRT tokens to guarantee they accomplish their jobs properly. If an indexer submits false data or indexes poorly, a portion of their stake may be reduced. Curators must stake GRT tokens on a Subgraph bonding curve, which is the curatorial signal utilized by indexes, to guarantee that they are steering indexes to the highest quality material. The major point is that the bonding curve encourages curators to be the first to bet on a new Subgraph that they feel has high-quality information. This is because curators receive a portion of the query fees paid to indexers, and curators who bet the most on a Subgraph being searched will receive a larger portion of the query fees assigned to curators due to the bonding curve. Although curators are not penalized for poor behavior in the same way that indexes are, they are subject to a withdrawal tax if they sell their interest in a Subgraph.

This is to ensure that they are committed to the network and to discovering the best quality Subgraphs, as picking a poor quality Subgraph results in no querying fees and a hefty withdrawal tax. Indexers, delegators, and curators also benefit from the rebate pool, which distributes GRT to those who contribute the most to the Graph network. Finally, any GRT staked by indexers, delegators, or curators is subject to a 20-day unlock period known as "the thawing phase." All of this sounds fantastic, but what does it all imply for the GRT token? GRT, on the other hand, is an ERC20 token with a total supply of 10 billion. It has a 3% annual inflation rate and is used to award indexing incentives to indexes. However, one percent of all query costs are used to burn GRT. The withdrawal fee imposed to curators is likewise burnt, as are any unclaimed rebate pool awards provided to network participants. This indicates that if there are enough query queries on the Graph Explorer, GRT might possibly become deflationary. Only 4% of GRT's original supply of 10 billion were sold at the Graphs ICO, which took place in October 2020.

This resulted in 400 million GRT being sold for 3 cents apiece, netting a profit of $12 million. It's worth mentioning that each individual participant in this ICO has a $5,000 investment cap. Those that participated in the ICO earned a comfortable 20x return on their investment and can now trade the token on extremely liquid markets like Coinbase, Binance, and a slew of other respected exchanges. Prior to the ICO, 200 million GRT were sold for 2.6 cents each to indexes and active community members, raising an additional 5.2 million dollars. Since its inception, The Graph has secured an additional $7.6 million in funding from a variety of investors, including Coinbase Ventures. These businesses got approximately 34% of the original supply of GRT, which was 3.4

billion GRT. To present, the Graph has raised around $25 million dollars. The remaining amount of GRT's initial supply has been allocated as follows: 23% to early project team members and advisors, 8% to Edge and Node, the new name of Graph protocol incorporated, the company that developed the Graph, and the remaining 29% to various community incentives, primarily the Graph foundation. Except for those sold during the ICO, all tokens are subject to various unlocking timelines that range from 6 months to 10 years. The majority of this vesting appears to be taking place within the next two years, with the total number of GRT tokens in circulation likely to treble in only six months. To put it bluntly, this is most likely the second worst token emission schedule in recent memory. The worst is the Solana's Soul token's emission timetable.

A 300 percent rise in supplies in only six months is, to put it mildly, astonishing. Even with the current bull run's increase in demand, I believe it will be difficult for GRT to see any meaningful price action with this flood of supply. However, circulating supply isn't the only factor influencing the GRT token's price in the future. What the Graph intends to accomplish in the following months and years will also be considered. Despite the fact that the GRT token will only be available in the market in December 2020, the Graph has been working with crypto projects for well over a year. Developers at Uniswap, Synthetics, Decentraland, Aragon, and other companies use the Graphs data protocol.

The Graph even constructed its first Dap, Everest, which is a registration for Ethereum-based decentralized apps. So far, over 3000 Subgraphs have been posted on the Graph Explorer, and the Graph network processes around half a billion data searches every day. The Graph's code was recently inspected by Open Zeppelin Trail of Bits and Consensus Diligence. The Graph Explorer is now hosted, or controlled, but will become a decentralized application on Ethereum in 2022. The launch of the Graph mainnet on December 17th, 2020, marked the beginning of a new era for the project. This marks the start of a shift to what appears to be a decentralized autonomous organization or DAO. The Graph foundation, whose aim is to create and preserve the Graph network, and the Graph council, which will monitor protocol governance, will be involved in this transitional phase. Furthermore, the Graph foundation will be legally and financially responsible to the Graph council. The Graph council is made up of ten people who represent the Graph's five stakeholder groups: indexes, users, researchers, backers, and the founding crew. These ten people will have the keys to a 6 of 10 multi-sig wallet that will manage cash used to support development grants awarded by the Graph foundation.

Who receives these scholarships will be determined by a community vote, and while the conditions have yet to be stated, I'm thinking that GRT token holders will be eligible. GRT token holders will be able to vote on issues such as the GRT token's inflation rate, what proportion of query fees are used to burn GRT, and how much GRT would be burnt by the curator withdrawal tax. Once this government system is in place, the Graph will add another network player known as a fisherman, who will be able to challenge the quality of on-chain data given by an indexer. Something that is presently being worked on by the Graph's development team. The last imminent milestone identified by the Graph is also the most crucial, and that is to spread beyond Ethereum to other blockchains. Although Ethereum is now the undisputed king of decentralized apps, there's no telling what a protocol like the Graph may do to improve other smart contract blockchains.

At the end of the day, anything that enhances decentralized apps is beneficial to the bitcoin sector, regardless of whose chain they are on. What the Graph provides and will bring to the table may be the deciding factor in cryptocurrency's eventual replacement of centralized institutions. All of the excitement over the Graph appears to be warranted. The Graph, like many other initiatives in the crypto sector, was driven by a dislike for the centralized manner of doing things. Recognizing the severe hazards of centralized data servers, which underpin nearly every service we use today, three bright individuals decided to develop a protocol.

A protocol for efficiently combing through decentralized data, hence supercharging current DAPps and speeding the rate at which new ones may be constructed. All of this is possible because the Graph Explorer, serves as a marketplace for data sets to which anybody may contribute and seek information. To ensure fair pricing, good quality data, and short fetching times, the Graph has devised a complex economic incentive system involving indexers who discover the data, delegators who ensure indexers are effective and inexpensive, and curators who develop and vet the data indexers are looking for. The GRT token, which is crucial to this incentive structure, would have ideal tokenomics if it didn't have a lack of community allocation and a cruel vesting schedule that will treble its circulating quantity in six months. However, something tells me that early investors are not moaning, considering that the GRT token has witnessed a 20x increase from its ICO pricing and likely still has the potential to rise before this major supply surge.

After all, the Graph main net was just recently published, and it has already demonstrated its worth and utility. With over 3000 Subgraphs, half a billion data searches each day, and some of the major cryptocurrency projects employing its technology to construct and improve their protocols. The Graph is in an excellent position to continue its spread onto other cryptocurrency blockchains. Going future, the Graph intends to further its decentralization efforts by establishing a non-profit foundation and a representative council that will eventually transfer the protocol to a Dow managed by GRT token holders. Regardless of the GRT token's present or future worth, the importance of what the Graph is bringing to the cryptocurrency industry cannot be overstated. Serverless data and genuinely decentralized apps will triumph over their centralized rivals.

CHAPTER 15:

HOW TO KEEP YOUR CRYPTO INVESTMENTS SAFE

In this chapter, I'll go through the Ledger Nano hardware wallet. This is also one of the greatest hardware wallets I've come across. You may use numerous software wallets for free right immediately, and you should probably do so as your first wallet. Hot wallets, on the other hand, are not secure when it comes to investing, especially significant sums of money. As a result, I would only propose a little amount, such as $100, as your initial investment in hot wallets. Anything less than $500 is less appealing to hackers, but it doesn't guarantee your assets are secure on hot wallets. As a result, only spend what you are willing to lose if you are hacked or lose your private keys.

To learn more about the Ledger Nano, click on https://www.ledger.com/. Once on the side, click on Crypto assets to get a list of all the cryptocurrencies supported by the Ledger Nano. Bitcoin, Bitcoin cash, Monero, Bitcoin Gold, Ethereum, Ethereum classic, Litecoin, Dogecoin, Zcash, XRP, Dash, Stratis, Komodo, Ark, Expanse, UBIQ, Vertcoin, Viacoin, Neo, Stealthcoin, Stellar, H-cash, Digibyte, Qtom, Pivx, and more cryptocurrencies are supported by the Ledger Nano. The Ledger supports several fantastic coins, however, some of them are absolutely useless. There are several reasons why I consider the Ledger Nano to be one of the greatest hardware wallets. For example, if you look at any of the coins supported by the Ledger, you will notice that they are also offering supplementary documentation for each token or cryptocurrency. If you look at the Bitcoin documentation, for example, it covers how to access setup, and debug the Bitcoin

Chrome application. When you click on it, you'll be taken to the table of contents, where you can see that they have a tutorial for everything. There are other really useful tutorials, such as HOW TO BUY BITCOINS, which explains what you need to do step by step, but you may also make requests or read relevant articles. There are also recently read articles and comments on many of the lessons. If you return to their home website and click on "chapters," then choose the device for which you want to see further chapters, you may get a variety of how-to tutorials. For example, how to create a new device, traverse the dashboard, transmit Bitcoins, recover a configuration, reset the device, send ethers, and so on, so you know all there is to know about the device, which is quite useful.

To purchase a Ledger Nano, go to "products" and pick the device you want to review, or you can just go to "compare our devices" and compare both their products, the Ledger Nano S and the Ledger Nano X. These gadgets are now available for $69 for the Nano S and $119 for the Nano X. The Nano S is their best-selling model, and it was also their first product to hit the market in 2014. My advice is to opt for a Nano S, and if you want to buy it, simply click "add to cart" and check the shipment schedule, as you may find that they can only deliver within 2 months, which is a long time, but the demand for these devices is really strong. Next, if you click "add to cart," then "checkout," you'll notice that they accept Bitcoins as a payment method, which is fantastic. When it came to delivery, the Ledger Nano S was no different than the Trezor in my instance.

The equipment did not come for approximately 6 weeks. When I purchased the ledger at the time, it was also less expensive. The Ledger Nano S, on the other hand, cost only 59 Euro, which included VAT. I had to pay extra 16 Euros for UPS delivery on top of the postal price, for a total of 75 Euros. A few months later, I purchased another Nano S as a backup as my savings account, but due to extremely high demand, I only received it 8 weeks after placing the order. The ledger firm is situated in Paris, France, so depending on where you live, you may receive it sooner than I did. If you don't want to wait weeks, you may check Amazon to see if they have it in stock, but it will most likely be more costly. When I was ready to buy a hardware wallet, I tried to buy it on Amazon, but even though the gadget was more expensive, Amazon was out of stock. If you're in a hurry and just want to use a Hardware wallet right away, I'd recommend checking Amazon first because you could get it a lot faster - assuming they have it in stock, of course. When it comes to building quality, I would recommend the Ledger Nano since it has the resilience to withstand the weight of a car.

The Ledger business not only says this, but my buddy tested it with his Fiat, which he videotaped and showed me, and I can confirm that it is actually quite powerful. My final tip is that you have a cold wallet so that you cannot be hacked, and the Ledger Nano S is ideal for this.

When purchasing the Nano from their website, no additional VAT costs are added to the price, and I believe it also looks much nicer. It's essentially a matter of personal choice. The Nano S is less costly than the Nano X or the Trezor, but more expensive than the KeepKey. If you decide to get a Leger Nano S or if you already own one and want to set it up for the first time, this tutorial will assist you. First and foremost, please go to https://www.ledger.com/start, where you will find four different stages. "Get Ledger Live to begin setting up your device" is the first step. "Select a PIN code and put down your recovery phrase" is the second step. "Install programs on your smartphone" is the third step. Step 4 is titled "Add an account to handle your cryptocurrency." So, in a word, you'll download the ledger live app, establish your pin and recovery phrase, install the programs on your ledger, and then add an account to manage your cryptocurrency. In its most basic form, that's exactly what it is. When you click on "download ledger live app," you will be presented with options for Windows, Mac, Linux, the App Store, and the Google Play Store. Once you've decided on an operating system, click the "download app" button. Once you've downloaded the app, proceed to step two and connect your smartphone via USB connection. When you put in your device, you will get a "welcome to ledger nano" message on the screen. On the device facing you, there are two buttons on the top, one on the left and one on the right.

To confirm your decision, you must press both buttons simultaneously. But first, you must press the right button to display the menu selections, or the left button to return to the last menu item you have just seen. You will be presented with several alternatives, and once you see "set up as a new device," you must press both buttons to approve it. If you continue to press the right or left buttons on the device, it will show you additional options such as "restore from recovery phrase," which is not what you want, so keep pushing the right/left buttons until you reach the menu option called "set up as a new device," and then press both buttons to select this menu option.

Next, your device's screen will display "Choose PIN code," so press both buttons once again to pick this menu option. When you get to this level, you must construct your pin code, and the device will ask you to confirm the pin code again in order to validate it. When finished, the gadget will say, "Write down your recovery phrase." You will only have one choice here, which is to press the button on the right, which will display the first recovery phrase that you must write down. You must repeat this step 24 times in order to view all of your recovery phrases on your smartphone and write them all down on the Recovery Sheet. After you've completed all 24 words, you'll see the following message on the gadget that says "tap left to validate your words." When you choose it, it will say "confirm your recovery phrase." At this point, you must confirm by selecting both buttons at the same time, which will ask you to "confirm word one" and then it will cycle through all 24 words for which you must confirm before moving on to the next step. Once you've validated all 24 words, which are your sole backup, save them in a safe location and never share them with anybody.

At this point, the device will display "push both buttons to continue," and it will begin processing your device. The device will then display "your device is now ready," with the option to click only the right button, followed by "press both buttons to access dashboard." Once completed, you will be within the Ledger as a newly configured device, where you may travel through the menu options until you reach the "install app" menu, then pick "Open ledger live to install applications." If you want to check what other options you have, you may go left or right to discover options such as "settings," where you will see further options such as "display," where you can adjust your display settings.

There is also a "security" or "firmware" option where you can examine the firmware version or if you want to "update your PIN," "password," or "reset all." You may test it out to see how it works. If you choose "reset all" on your device, you will be able to generate a new fresh ledger. These are additional options to be aware of, however, in order to complete the setup of your device, you must select "push both buttons to access dashboard." When you are on ledger live on your computer screen, you will get a message that says "Welcome to Ledger Live," and you will be able to choose whether the application should operate in light, dusk, or dark mode. Once you've decided, click "get started" and then "set up as new device." Next, choose your device, which in this example is the Nano S, and then click "proceed." The following page will be labeled "security checklist," and it will ask you the following questions: "1. Did you pick your pin code on your own?" "2. Did you create your own recovery phrase? "3 Is your ledger device authentic?" You can choose a yes or no response for each of these questions. When you answer question number three, "Is your ledger device genuine?" you will be prompted to check now and asked to "connect and unlock your device."

At this point, you must insert your pin into your device and then press both buttons to enable the ledger manager on your smartphone. When finished, you should see the message "Device is authentic," then click "proceed." The following screen is titled "password lock," and it is optional, but it allows you to establish a password to restrict unwanted access to Ledger Live data on your computer, such as account names, transactions, and public addresses. Following the selection and confirmation of a password, the following screen will state: "Bugs and analytics." This is where you may choose what you want with analytics and bug reports if you want to share information with a Ledger firm to help them address issues, but it's optional, so once you're ready to go on, simply pick "continue."

The following screen will indicate "your device is ready!" and will have an option to "open ledger live." When you click it, you'll be sent to your platform's menu options on the right, which include "portfolio," "Accounts," "Send," "Receive," "Manager," and "Buy Crypto." If you select "portfolio," you will be required to "enable ledger manager on your device," which means you must press both buttons on your Nano device to access your portfolio. Once completed, Ledger Live will detect your Ledger Nano S and provide extra information that you have not before seen.

The firmware version number, how much space is consumed, and what the entire capacity of the device is, as well as an option for "app catalog" and "apps installed" will be displayed. Within the "app catalog" option, you will notice various cryptocurrencies, with another option named "Install" next to each, which you must click on to acquire a wallet. When the installation is finished, you will see the word "installed," but each time you install a new bitcoin wallet, you must keep track of how much space you have used on the hardware. You don't have to be concerned about them because you can view how much space each cryptocurrency wallet requires as well as how much space you have remaining. For the Ledger Nano S, you should expect to receive 3 to 6 wallets on average.

Assuming you have downloaded the Bitcoin app, the next step is to add a Bitcoin account. To do so, select "add account" and then "proceed." At this point, you will be invited to confirm it on your smartphone by pressing both buttons simultaneously. Following that, you will notice that it is synchronizing, and once validated, you must click on "close." You may use the same method to download and add accounts to other cryptocurrencies. The Ledger Nano is also capable of numerous capabilities, but that is it in a nutshell. Your Ledger Nano S is now ready to accept and transfer Bitcoins and other cryptocurrencies.

The Ledger Nano X is the company's most recent product, and it has several improvements over the previous generation, the Nano S. The key improvements are the bigger digital display and the placement of the two buttons on the front rather than the top. It's a little more durable and heavier, but the amount of programs you can install has been substantially enhanced. The previous legend used to fill up with three or four application wallets, which isn't ideal if you have a lot of various coins. The Nano X can accommodate over a hundred apps, so talk about how to get everything set up.

First and foremost, ensure that you have purchased one from the official website and that you have not acquired a used gadget, since there are many fraudsters out there attempting to take advantage of you. Also, be certain that everything arrives in its original packing. The Nano X can be connected to a computer, but it also has a Bluetooth enabled capability. The first step is to download and install the ledger live up from the website https://www.ledger.com/ledger-live/download. Once there, click "Download" and select the operating system on which you wish to utilize the Ledger Live App. The official Ledger website indicates that you can obtain the ledger live app on your phone and then link it with Bluetooth and use it that way as well, but I still believe that using the wire is the easiest method to set it up on your computer, at least the first time. Simply launch the Ledger Live App after downloading it and select "get started." If you've written down your backup phrases, you may restore it from an old device here. If you have the backup phrases saved safely and you lose your ledger, it breaks for any reason, or you simply want to transfer your old ledger information to the new device, this is where you may restore it.

But first, I'll show you how to set it up for the first time. So, after clicking "Get Started," you'll be given the alternatives "Initialize as a new device," "Restore device from recovery phrase," and "Use an initialised device." Here, you'll want to select "Initialize as a new device." Then, pick "Ledger Nano X" and press the "proceed" button. The next page will instruct you to go to your device and begin setting up a PIN number. On your Nano X, you may change the digits by pressing the right or left button, and you can confirm your pin numbers by pressing both buttons at the same time.

As a new device, it will prompt you to enter a four or eight digit PIN number; nevertheless, please remember that you should never disclose that information with anybody. After that, you must confirm the pin number for the second time, and you will be asked to put down your recovery phrase. It is critical that you write down all 24 words in the exact sequence in this stage. The most significant aspect is that this is your final backup. If something goes wrong and you lose your ledger, you must have these 24 words to recover all of your Bitcoins. Once you've typed down those 24 words in the correct sequence on your recovery sheet, it'll just ask you to confirm them again. This is going to take some time, so don't rush it and don't make any mistakes. After you re-enter those 24 words, the gadget will say "processing" followed by "finished correctly." When you're finished, return to the Ledger Live App and select "continue." The following screen will ask you if you have written down your recovery phrase, and you can just click "yes" here. The next screen will question if you "chosen your PIN number yourself" and "saved your recovery phrase," so select "yes" for both. Then, in question 23, you'll be asked, "Is your Ledger device genuine?" and you'll be prompted to select "check now." This will double-check that you've done everything correctly thus far before telling you that "your gadget is authentic." When the security check is finished, click "proceed." The following page is only an optional setting called "Password lock," which adds another degree of protection.

This isn't for the Nano X gadget itself, but rather adds an additional layer of protection to your computer or phone. You can enter a new password here and then click "continue." On the next screen, you'll see "bug reports and analytics," in which you can choose to join but it's also optional, so once you've set your preferences, click "continue." The following screen will indicate "your device is ready," and you'll have a choice to "launch Ledger Live," which you should select. On the following screen, select the "open manager" menu option. This is done so that you may install the app and then create an account once it has been installed. To begin your initial installation, select the Bitcoin app and click "install." This is for installing a program on your phone or laptop, but once installed, you must add an account to it, which is an address for your Bitcoin.

Just because you have the app doesn't imply you have an account set up, thus this is a two-step procedure that many people get mixed up about. After you've loaded the Bitcoin App, you may install a plethora of other cryptocurrency apps because the Nano X has far greater storage capacity than the Nano S. Furthermore when you download bitcoin applications, you will notice that the Nano X is far quicker than the Nano S. After you've installed all of the applications that require an address, you must go to "accounts" and add an account. For example, suppose you've installed the Bitcoin app and want to set up a Bitcoin account for it. So, if you put "Bitcoin" into the necessary form and then choose the asset, it will ask you to browse to your Bitcoin app on the digital display and then click on both buttons. Then, select "continue," and it will sync up.

This shouldn't take too long, but the first time you do it will take a little longer than the second time. This is the process of creating a Bitcoin account and an address for yourself. Following that, you'll see that you've "successfully added a Bitcoin account." For example, if you want to create a Litecoin account, it will not allow you to add a point account since you have not yet loaded the Litecoin software through the manager in the ledger live. So, if you wish to add other accounts for other cryptocurrencies, you must first install those apps. Once you've made an account in ledger live management, you may click on "Bitcoin" and then "receive." This will need you to open the Bitcoin app on your device and tap both buttons. When this opens, it will only ask you to verify the address on our device, so click "proceed." This will display your Bitcoin address on your computer screen, as well as the same address on the display screen of your Nano X.

If you're new to bitcoin and have just purchased some for the first time, here is the address to which you should transfer your Bitcoins. Rather than the exchange, it may be safely saved on your smartphone. You can copy this and then paste it somewhere, such as the exchange or wherever you are sending your Bitcoins. The procedure is the same for any other cryptocurrency. Simply go into the manager, install more applications, and then set up an account. With the various cryptocurrency wallets, you may call those accounts whatever you like, and then you construct an address to keep them safe. Hopefully, that's a clear and simple explanation. Now, let's look at how to upgrade your Ledger Nano, whether it's a S or an X. I know some folks were terrified when they updated the newest upgrades and then saw that their Bitcoins were vanished from their hardware wallet. However, they failed to reinstall the applications and reconnect their connected account to the wallet. So, to avoid misunderstanding, let's go through the firmware upgrading process step by step. You must first launch Ledger Live, and after it is launched, you will notice a notification at the top of your screen reading "ledger live 2.9.0 is ready for an update," with the option to "Download now" on the side. After you click "Download Now," it will begin downloading the most recent software, and when it is finished, you will get a notification that says "Update ready to install" and "install now" on the side. When you click "install now," it will reset itself, requiring you to enter your password again, and a new pop-up window labeled "release notes" will appear.

This will display a list of new features and recent problem fixes, which you may read before clicking "continue." The update is now complete, but if you want to double-check it, go to "settings" and then "about," where you'll find the Version number. Click "Details" to ensure that you have the most recent version installed. Then you'll want to check your Nano S or Nano X, which you'll need to connect in before going to "manager." You must also enter your pin code to unlock your device, and once in the management part of your ledger Nano, you will see 1.2.4-1 as the firmware on your ledger Nano. You may notice a different version while reading this book, and you should also see at the top of your screen that "firmware version 1.2.4-2 is available," as well as an option to "upgrade firmware" on the side. To update that firmware, click on it, which will bring up another popup window with the firmware upgrade instructions, but also with a warning reading "I have my recovery phrase." You must check that box and then click "continue."

The upgrade will then take a few minutes to finish, so be patient. Before the download window reaches 100% completion, your Nano will ask you to confirm a special code physically on the device, which you must do first. Once validated, you will see a notification on your computer screen that says "device in Bootloader mode." To amend it, click Continue." Here, you must hit "proceed," and your Nano will display "boot loader mode" in the meanwhile. It is critical that you do not unplug your device at this stage, as you might easily screw up the entire firmware upgrade. When finished, it will state "firmware upgraded, please reinstall the apps on your smartphone." You must now unlock your Nano and enter the pin code. Then, on the Bitcoin applications or any other apps that you already had on your Nano, click "install." Once the applications are loaded, go to "manage my accounts" and click "add an account," then pick Bitcoin or any other account you previously had in a manner similar to how you would set up your smartphone the first time.

It's very self-explanatory; just pick continue, update, and enter your pin code correctly, and you're ready to go. From then, as previously said, always keep your recovery phrase backed up. You can do this by using the cards that come with your Nano and keeping them secure. Keep things hidden so you can bring them out and double-check everything on your Nano. You never want to lose those recovery phrases because it will result in the loss of your crypto assets. Also, if the firmware upgrade fails, Ledger will gladly provide you with hardware, but you will lose access to your cryptocurrencies if you do not have your recovery phrases. Always remember that you are your own bank, and you must double-check and verify everything to ensure that it is absolutely secure.

CPSIA information can be obtained
at www.ICGtesting.com
Printed in the USA
BVHW060221200722
642495BV00009B/778